Teaching

Writing

in a **TITLE I** School

The Name

He didn't want to work that hard,
and she knew it.
So she brushed a tired, ageless lock of hair from
her eyes, tucked it up

and bent over
the small scratched desk.
with his hand in hers.

"Like this," she breathed softly,

her hand over his small
soft one.

He trembled a small *j*
then an *o*
a crooked *s*
the lop-sided *e.*

It was enough,
for today. But she knew
looking down, that writing only
a name

would never be enough at all.

K–3

Teaching *Writing* in a **TITLE I** School

Nancy Akhavan

HEINEMANN
Portsmouth, NH

Heinemann
361 Hanover Street
Portsmouth, NH 03801–3912
www.heinemann.com

Offices and agents throughout the world

The author and publisher wish to thank those who have generously given permission to reprint borrowed material:

Adapted from "List of 100 Most Frequently Used Words" from *The Reading Teacher's Book of Lists, Fifth Edition* by Edward B. Fry, Ph.D. and Jacqueline E. Kress, Ed.D. Copyright © 2006 by Jon Wiley & Sons, Inc. Published by Jossey-Bass. Reprinted by permission of Jon Wiley & Sons, Inc.

Library of Congress Cataloging-in-Publication Data
Akhavan, Nancy L.
   Teaching writing in a Title I school, K–3 / Nancy Akhavan.
       p. cm.
   Includes bibliographical references and index.
   ISBN-13: 978-0-325-01388-6
   ISBN-10: 0-325-01388-8
   1. English language—Composition and exercises—Study and teaching (Elementary). 2. Report writing—Study and teaching (Elementary). 3. Children with social disabilities—Education—United States. 4. Federal aid to education—United States. I. Title. II. Title: Teaching writing in Title One schools, K–3.

LB1576.A399 2009
372.62'3—dc22   2009015374

Editor: Lisa Luedeke
Production: Lynne Costa
Cover design: Shawn Girsgerger
Typesetter: Val Levy, Drawing Board Studios
Manufacturing: Valerie Cooper

Printed in the United States of America on acid-free paper

13 12 11 10 09   VP   1 2 3 4 5

Dedicated to
Cindy Tucker
for being an extraordinary mentor and
allowing your life light to show the way to
truth and resilience.

Contents

Appendix

Acknowledgments

This book began with a summer phone call. It was one of those phone calls that changes everything you think about your work and your passions. Thank you to my editor, Lisa Luedeke, and Maura Sullivan of Heinemann who made that phone call and tapped me to write this book. I dreamed this dream because of their focus and ingenuity.

Since that summer day when Lisa and Maura called me, I have been on a journey that has put me in touch with hundreds of people. For the last two years I have worked for Fresno Unified School District, the fourth largest district in California. I thank all the individuals and teachers who prodded me to frame a writing book for teachers working in Title I schools. There are hundreds of you and too many to mention. Thank you to all of you for your open arms, for openly sharing your thinking, and your teaching.

I am also grateful to the primary teachers at Lee Richmond Elementary School and Pinedale Elementary School who graciously shared their classrooms with me. This book wouldn't exist without your focus on instruction, belief in children, and willingness to share student writing and teaching charts.

Thank you to Val Hogwood, Deanna Mathies, Pamela Pflepsen, and Hollie Olsen for helping me think through lessons, student literacy needs, and best practices. Thank you also for believing in kids so that we can all grow together.

Team Heinemann continues to support my writing and work in a way that helps me dream dreams for touching the lives of many teachers and students. I am blessed to work with a fabulous team that hopes for extraordinary resources for educators and helps those resources come alive. Thank you to all of you for your continued support and the magic you work every day. I am especially appreciative of Lisa Luedeke for listening and advising expertly during book development, Maura Sullivan for shaping proposals and ideas, Lynne Costa for carefully taking care of this manuscript with the plethora of figures and photographs, and Alan Huisman for his expertise in editing.

Of course, I am forever indebted to my husband who asks me each day: "What will you write today?"

Introduction

Three words currently on the lips of many teachers—*engagement, learning, intervention*—represent a myriad of meanings, successes, and pressures.

Engagement means students are participating in the lesson and are learning. It implies some things not necessarily apparent. Sometimes our students are not engaged by our teaching; they are sitting by, letting others in class do the learning while they remain on the emotional and intellectual periphery. As teachers, we might need to leave our favorite teaching style behind and focus on student learning styles. Student engagement also requires that we examine our values and introduce new things, including best practices, in our daily instruction.

Learning denotes that students know something they did not previously know. For those of us teaching every day, this word, too, has implications beyond its obvious definition. One aspect of student learning is captured in test scores on standardized tests that match expectations in state and federal guidelines. Specifically, student learning is measured in accordance with edicts in the No Child Left Behind legislation. But *learning* also means that we have introduced effective literacy practices to our students and taught them how to implement them. There is a lot to balance as we learn new teaching practices, run to keep up with the pace of the school year, follow assessment calendars, oversee projects, and fulfill extracurricular responsibilities.

Intervention encompasses the actions we take to ensure that all students learn the material they are expected to learn. In other words, students enter our classrooms at different skill and knowledge levels, and we have to provide opportunities for them to learn material based on their needs—no small task. The heart of intervention is understanding that student learning is also our responsibility as teachers, not solely the students' responsibility.

We have to engage students, teach for learning, and intervene if children are not learning.

If you are teaching in a Title I school, a school that serves a high proportion of children receiving assistance through the free and reduced-price lunch program, you are also probably serving children who need additional time to learn academic material, because their home and community experiences are unique and very different from their school experiences. They may have responsibilities that leave little time for studying and homework. Their role models may be older brothers, sisters, cousins, or neighborhood friends who feel school isn't for them; it's just a place they have to attend for a while, not a key training station in becoming an adult. Some of these children are probably learning English.

Despite these special issues and student needs, teaching in a Title I school is a deeply rewarding experience. Each year I would set up my classroom, lovingly place my favorite books where they had the best chance of enticing students, listen to students read with glee and amazement at their newfound skill, and read their writing. Hearing their voices develop, I knew I had found my calling.

In *Teaching Reading in a Title I School, K–3* (2008), I explain how to infuse your classroom with effective reading practices that can help you focus on improving student performance while meeting state standards and addressing mandates. But reading is only one set of literacy skills a young child needs to develop early and well. The other set, writing, is rarely taught. Writing is often *assigned*, but children are not taught *how* to write. Writing is often pulled apart into bits and pieces of skills but not taught as an integrated, organic process.

Writing is a gatekeeping skill. Those students who write well do well in the upper-elementary grades, in high school, and beyond. Those who are never given the opportunity to learn to write never get the chance to think, connect, and excel in classes that demand of them the ability to show what they know. Writing *must* be taught in the primary grades; primary teachers build the foundation for the highly developed writing and genre explorations children engage in later on. The first writing steps we provide our students are essential.

Passion as a Reason to Focus

It had been a long day. I had driven four hours to get to the conference in Northern California, spent several hours attending sessions, then scrambled across the convention center, weaving through the crowds, to get to the room assigned to me for my late-day presentation. The teachers who gathered in the room looked both exhausted and hopeful. I began my talk about helping young children, particularly English learners, write. I laid the first piece of student work onto the overhead and read it aloud, and then I talked about writing workshop and the power of having children write every day. A participant raised her hand: "How does this apply to me? How can I possibly teach writing when I have to cover so much in the reading textbook? This has no meaning for me."

That teacher felt compelled. She felt compelled to attend a session to help her teach writing to her students. She felt compelled to learn how to become a teacher of writing. She felt compelled to ensure that her young students had the writing knowledge and skill they needed to be successful in subsequent grades and find pleasure in putting their thoughts on the page. She also felt compelled to follow the textbook her principal expected her to use. In the middle of all that compulsion, as well as to retain her sanity, it was easiest to walk away and say, "This has no meaning for me."

I have met hundreds of primary teachers in this same boat. They

- feel compelled to teach writing
- are befuddled by how to squeeze writing into an already too-full teaching day
- are afraid their students' test scores may fall if they spend time writing

    I tell them all the same thing:

- It's wonderful that you feel compelled to teach writing. You should, because it is the one thing that students don't have enough experience with; the one thing by which they can leave a permanent, public record of what they learn, process, and think about; the one thing that employers complain that their employees cannot do well; the one thing that students will have to do daily in college and in their careers; the one thing we learn best by teaching.
- If we don't carve out prominent space in our teaching day for writing, we are sending children onward without all the things I just listed.
- If students cannot comprehend, cannot think, and cannot learn well, their test scores will go down anyway.

Facing Difficulty and Pressing Forward Anyway

Teaching writing is difficult. It is even more difficult in a Title I school. Maybe your students come to school hungry and have to grab a quick breakfast in the cafeteria. Maybe when they go home, the house will be empty and cold while they wait for their parents to return from a long, hard workday. Perhaps they live with a grandma or grandpa whose resources are too meager to provide everything a young child needs.

So you come to work every day to make a difference, to make a home for these kids, to help them learn so they have a chance at being successful readers and writers. The first step you can take to help your students be successful is to teach them to write—writing is essential (Graham, MacArthur, and Fitzgerald 2007). Really. Teaching children to write well is the key to helping them express themselves well, a scaffold to guide their thinking and understanding. It just might be the silver bullet you seek that will solve your teaching problems, ensure that all children learn, and close the achievement gap. Well, *almost* a silver bullet. The act of writing demands what no other act demands of children: to produce, to create, to own, to think. The act of writing nurtures children's abilities to own information and ideas and then turn around and share that information, those ideas, with the world. Teaching writing increases children's ability to

- synthesize
- create
- think
- connect ideas
- connect thoughts to sounds and sounds to words
- comprehend
- know

Carl Nagin, in conjunction with the others in the National Writing Project (2006), writes, ". . . writing could develop higher-order thinking skills: analyzing, synthesizing, evaluating, and interpreting. The very difficulty of writing is its virtue . . ." (22). Writing helps students learn inquiry strategies for discovering, elaborating, and testing ideas. Through the act of writing, they discover better thought patterns, learn information, and share their ideas with others in the intensively collaborative world we now live in.

Therefore, regardless of the difficulties we face, we must teach writing to serve children well. This book will answer some of the questions facing you as you launch writing instruction in your classroom. It discusses issues facing you as a Title I teacher focusing on writing in the primary grades.

Perhaps you are wondering how to fit writing workshop into your day. Perhaps you are wondering why you should teach writing in a literacy block (like a workshop) or why you should teach genre projects (Hansen 2001). Why not just teach writing prompts or give on-demand writing assessments after a bit of instruction? Because it is important to teach in a context in which you can *engage* your students, ensure *learning*, and *intervene* when children are not learning (Chall 2000; National Writing Project and Nagin 2006).

The Teaching Imperative: Engage, Teach, Intervene

You cannot intervene and reteach if you don't know what and how students are supposed to be learning, what they should be writing and how. Organizing writing instruction by genre and thinking of every few weeks of instruction as a unit in which you will develop a particular genre gives you a perfect opportunity to fold in writing skills, genre characteristics, and the components of the writing process. When you organize instruction around units of study, you can use lessons from whatever writing program your school or district has adopted. You can teach writing without a writing program as well, focusing your instruction on standards and specific writing skills that may be embedded in your adopted reading program. Organizing writing instruction by genre also allows you to *assess for learning*—that is, conduct coordinated assessments that you then use to plan lessons—rather than measure learning after teaching.

Organizing instruction in units of study is conducive to intervention (Donovan and Smolkin 2006). When it is clear what students are to learn and what they will create to show what they have learned, you can plainly see where to intervene and reteach. Using units of study makes it much easier to team-teach students with similar learning needs, teach specific lessons to small groups, or hold an after-school session for children who need extra time. If you think of intervention as reteaching, or added teaching, then really good first teaching will decrease the amount of intervention you need to do. To that end, you can scaffold your initial minilessons so that more students grasp more ideas and concepts right away.

Be yourself when you teach. Celebrate what your students can do, not what they cannot do. Explicitly show your students how a writing strategy works, how one genre is different from another, or how to have the writing stamina to keep writing even when it is difficult. If you do, your students will write moving pieces that will pull at your heartstrings (like Darion's narrative in Figure I.1); they will write to inform; they will write to learn. Teach writing so your students own *how* to write. Take the advice of Donald Murray (2004), a great writer and teacher of writing: don't teach the way you think I would teach, or the way your best friend teaches. Teach it your way; teach like yourself.

FIGURE I.1   Darion's Narrative

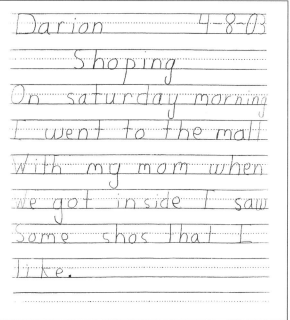

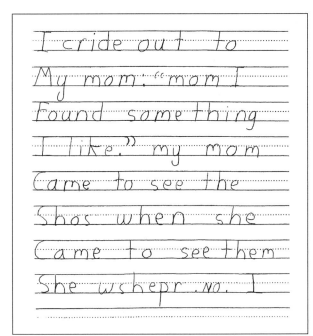

FIGURE I.1 Darion's Narrative (*continued*)

I cride out to
My mom. "mom I
Found something
I like." my mom
Came to see the
Shos when she
Came to see them
She wshepr. no. I

felt mad. Frst I
Whined. then I
bretend to cri
for the shos. Next
I stoop my foot.
Finally she yelled
Out "o.k I will
buy them if

You stop that"
O.k. I crid out
to my mom". when
she bought the
shos I wshepr
to my self I have
a grate mom.

PART 1

Engage

The beginning of this book is designed to help you understand a child's writing ability and performance as he or she develops over time, consider the writing growth and development of children, and see how this growth develops in a continuum. Children grow and learn in spurts and plateaus; the wonder of guiding this growth is understanding what they need to learn overall and to plan appropriate lessons when children are struggling.

These first three chapters will help you gather a snapshot of what writing instruction may look like when tailored to engage children's curiosity and imagination and then guide them to success by helping your young students learn to put their ideas on paper. Very young children use temporary spelling, also known as *invented spelling*, when they write down their thoughts. This temporary spelling counts. It takes some time before children are able to spell words conventionally. More words in a piece don't necessarily make the writing better, but when children are struggling to write anything at all, understanding how to guide their development is important (Clay 2001).

Learning and growth is cyclical and not linear—not for your students or for you as you develop your teaching practices. May you thrive as your students learn, and may you find joy in teaching your children to write.

CHAPTER ONE

Engagement Strategies for Working with Young Writers

It's 9:05 A.M. and the campus is quiet. As I stroll from the upper-grade wing to the primary wing, a warm breeze rustles the leaves in the large, sprawling mulberry trees that guard the first- and second-grade classroom doors like knights waiting for their young pages.

I peek into the small square glass window in the door of room 6, at Kristina Karlson's first-grade class. This room is not quiet. It is filled with the sound of learning, bustling with children busy with literacy. Children are writing, looking at pieces in their folders, thinking aloud as their fingertips slide across pages filled with large, scrawling print. Some children patter across the floor to the storage area, grab some more paper, stride back to their desks, and resume writing. I watch as large pencils made for small hands move across pieces of paper. I can almost hear the scritch-scratch as the children fill page after page with the wonder of words.

These first graders are busy. They think they are writing, but in actuality they are expressing themselves and making letter-sound and thought-word connections; their early spelling attempts show the world they have ideas and can think. These first graders are excited; they value their own and their classmates' ideas and writing. Acceptance and anticipation hang in the air as I enter the classroom. It is contagious; I can't wait to read what the children have worked on, give a high five to an eager young writer. I can't wait to congratulate Kristina, who has worked so hard to ensure that these children have the world of opportunity at their feet. This world of opportunity didn't happen by accident. Kristina has carefully crafted an environment in which each child is engaged and active.

Motivation and Student Engagement

Motivation and engagement go hand in hand. When we are engaged, our brain is in gear. We are emotionally ready and committed to embark on a learning journey and work at it along the way (Guthrie and Wigfield 2000; Schunk and Zimmerman 2006). When the gears click, we are eager to undertake a new activity, tackle new learning; when they don't, we don't feel motivated to get anything done. Engagement means that our feelings and senses are tapped and tuned in to the present learning, that our attention is focused and we feel a need and reason to work at the task, that something is pulling us along to work and work harder (Brewster and Fager 2000).

One way to recognize engagement is to look at what children are doing in a classroom. Involved and engaged children initiate activities when given the opportunity, work with effort and concentration, and feel good about doing so (Barell 2003; Guthrie and Wigfield 2000). Skinner and Belmont (1991) define engagement in school as the intensity and emotional quality of children's involvement in initiating and carrying out learning activities. This intensity and emotion manifest themselves as enthusiasm, optimism, curiosity, and interest. Engaged children *want* to work hard. Engagement is triggered when you create invitations for involvement and scaffold the experiences so children can be successful.

Writing can be an invitation. Children who are able to express themselves find joy in learning; they think about the messages they write to share with friends and are often fully engaged in the writing process. One child might draw and label pictures (see Yadira's penguin report in Figure 1.1); another might share a memory by slowing the moment down and stretching out the details (see Darchea's narrative about her dad in Figure 1.2).

FIGURE 1.1   One Page from Yadira's Penguin Report

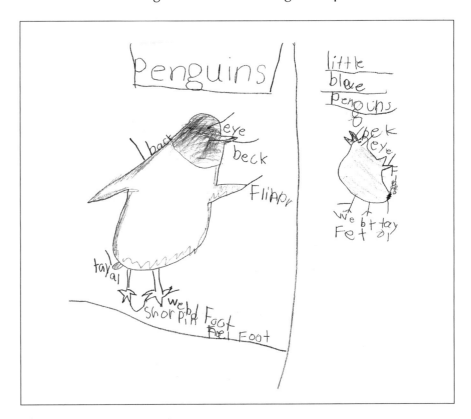

FIGURE 1.2 Darchea's Piece About a Moment with Her Dad

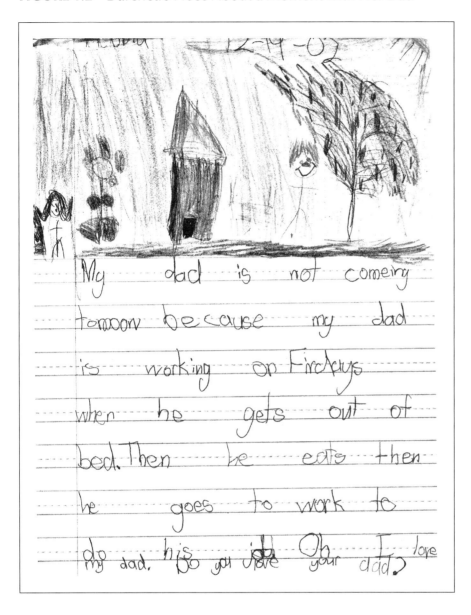

Find children's learning edge—that place between what they can do well alone and what they can do with help from a mentor, teacher, or adult—and you will motivate them to work. Vygotsky (1978) calls this the zone of proximal development. When a task is new and fresh and feels doable, a child will engage. When a task is new and fresh and feels insurmountable, a child will be disinterested in working hard. Focus on the learning edge and help children have cognitive clarity about what they are learning. Cognitive clarity makes a task doable (Barell 2003; Cunningham and Cunningham 2002).

Engagement Strategies

There is no bag of tricks for creating student engagement, nor can engagement be turned on or off at will or whim. But sometimes writing teachers approach engagement as if they can choose when to engage and disengage their students. When writing instruction is effective, children are always engaged. Specific things excellent writing teachers do *each and every day* to ensure student engagement include

- creating a classroom community
- teaching through process and product
- providing clear and explicit good first teaching
- offering opportunities to try and try again
- promoting active movement, physical and mental, throughout the classroom
- ensuring that children talk during the minilesson, while writing, and when sharing
- giving many opportunities for students to think throughout writing instruction, practice, and creation

Create a Classroom Community

A classroom with no focus, continuity, and connection is a scary place! For many years I never thought about the community I created for children, the atmosphere that permeated my classroom, or how my actions—my choices in furniture arrangement and wall color—affected the people who entered it each day. I never realized how these things affected me either.

Gradually it dawned on me. When the classroom was cluttered and my lessons were not clear, when I didn't stop inappropriate comments or actions made by students right away, I felt off base. I felt more competent and was infinitely more patient with my students when the atmosphere was inviting and engaging, when the classroom was well organized, comfortable, and cheery. Most important, my students treated each other with respect, and a sense of pleasant urgency to read and write was palpable. When my classroom community was effective, it promoted engagement.

Young children need the support of their peers and their teachers. They need to interact within a community of learners (Flores, Cousin, and Diaz 1991). Writing creates this community as students share their ideas out loud and go to one another for help with spelling or revision.

To establish this community, begin by emphasizing tolerance and acceptance. Expect all children to treat one another fairly and respectfully. Model fairness, and leave sarcasm at the door. Sarcasm may seem a way to play around with students and create a lighthearted atmosphere, but it isn't. Sarcasm is hurtful and sends a clear message that your classroom is not a safe place to be (Jensen 2000). Immediately point out inappropriate comments children make as well; don't let them put one another down.

FIGURE 1.3 Having Students Work Together Fosters Engagement and Respect

FIGURE 1.4 By Listening to and Learning From One Another, Students Learn to Tolerate New Ideas and Differences of Opinion

FIGURE 1.5 Classroom Community Checklist

Classroom Community Observation Checklist

School:_____   Room number:_____

Teacher:_____   Date:_____

Context for Instruction	
Room Environment	**Evidence**
Class meeting area is established.	
Room arrangement allows for whole-group instruction in meeting area.	
Room arrangement allows for small-group instruction and individual conferring.	
Corners of room provide space for writing partners to work together.	
Desk area allows for collaborative group work and sharing of materials.	
Materials and Resources	
Writing materials are accessible to children.	
Large amount of books in a variety of genres is available.	
Teaching charts are displayed and are current.	
Classroom walls teach and are filled with purposeful print.	
Teaching table has organized writing materials.	
Books represent diversity.	
Word wall, word banks, and vocabulary words are displayed and current.	
Student Interaction	
Students are respectful of one another's work and ideas.	
Students listen to each other and avoid put-downs.	
Behavioral expectations are posted.	
Teacher demonstrates routines and expectations.	

A caring, focused classroom community accepts mistakes and celebrates learning. Model this with your whole heart and all your energy. You can begin creating this focused, thoughtful atmosphere by using the checklist in Figure 1.5. A checklist doesn't capture the essence of community, of course, but it can help you think about and reflect on what is in place in your classroom and what might need a bit of modification.

- Review the classroom community checklist.
- Make one or two appropriate changes in your classroom.

Balance Process and Product

Before you ask children to begin writing in daily workshops, you need to make clear to them how the lesson you are presenting will shape their knowledge of writing *while they are writing*. In other words, they need to be aware of the product they are supposed to work on (the piece of writing) and the process they are to use to create it (planning, drafting, revising, editing, and publishing). When children know what is expected of them and are shown *how* to do something, they control their learning, and control equals connected, engaged students (Blankenstein 2004; Cunningham and Cunningham 2002).

Give children control of their learning by telling them

- what they are going to be writing
- why they are going to write
- how they are going to know their writing is good enough
- where they will work on their writing—alone, with a partner, in a small group

FIGURE 1.6 Jayden's Poem

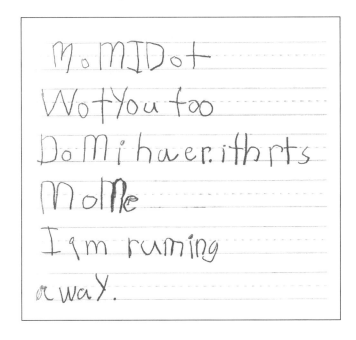

Defining what, why, how, and where creates a balanced synergy between what and why, how and where, because the children are constructing knowledge while writing (Cambourne 2002). What and why address the teaching goal; how and where address the teaching delivery. When children know what they are supposed to write, when you show them what this writing looks like, sounds like, and feels like (in the brain, in the heart, in the hand), you help children *own* their learning and encourage them to be curious, to work with desire and stamina. Eliminate ambiguity and your students will write and share their writing with purpose and pleasure; they will love writing and will work hard with curiosity and endurance (Spandel 2008).

When you eliminate ambiguity in your lessons and your assignments, you help children focus on and be responsible for their learning. For example, take Figure 1.6, Jayden's poem capturing a memory.

What and Why
Jayden clearly knew she was writing a poem—capturing a small moment (Calkins 2003). She knew what to do and did it. Her teacher's teaching point is clear in the work Jayden created. She knew how to write with detail. She also wrote to read her writing to her peers and her teacher. At the end of the workshop, Jayden picked up her piece and sat in the sharing circle, wriggling her tiny toes in her sandals, tapping her paper on the floor in front of her crossed legs. She beamed when it was her turn. She talked about her poem with the group. She knew she was supposed to add a detail, and she talked about how her poem had a detail the way "real" poems have details.

How and Where
Shana, Jayden's teacher, paused after taking a moment to appreciate the poem. She asked, "Do you think you could have added more? Remember how we said a small moment has details? Do you think your piece has enough details?" Shana pointed to the teaching chart from the minilesson. Jayden had a moment to reflect on her work and think about what she could have done differently. While all the children were gathered on the floor at the conclusion of the workshop (*where*), Shana retaught the point of the lesson by inquiring into Jayden's thinking and pointing to the chart to remind her of the objective (*what*).

- Focus on what point you want to teach and why you are teaching that particular point.
- Think about where and how you are going to deliver the instruction.
- Help students own their learning and the writing process.

Provide Good First Teaching
Every child deserves a close encounter with a very good teacher (Clay 2001). We can all be that very good teacher, that *great* teacher who ensures

students are learning the right stuff. Certain actions maximize children's opportunities to solve words and recognize genre characteristics and help them take control of their writing. Nothing is more powerful than having high expectations for what children can do. Don't assume that kindergartners can't write narratives or even informational reports just because they start school not knowing their alphabet. Children come to our classrooms filled with experiences they can write about and some awareness (however fledging) of the alphabetic principle. First and second graders will grow in their abilities to control language and thought and come to understand at least three genres: narrative writing, report writing, and procedural writing. By third grade, the children will have a more in-depth knowledge of these genres as well as be able to write a response to a literature selection.

Check your assumptions at the door:

- Avoid teaching detours (no "and then" lessons; see Akhavan 2004). Keep teacher talk to a minimum.
- Savor the unique characteristics of each child and see possibility in what he doesn't know as much as in what he can do.
- Simplify tasks, not content.

Try and Try Again

I began my first year of teaching with a group of thirty-two first graders, twenty-eight of whom were English learners. I didn't know what I was doing; thankfully, the children were young and didn't know what they were doing either. They were just glad to be in "big-kid school," no longer in kindergarten. Having now worked with children in five districts, at levels ranging from preschool to ninth grade, I know many things about working with diverse populations and about how children become literate.

But before I knew any of these things, I knew something more important: *the first time I try something, I rarely succeed*. I have to try, practice, revise, and try again when learning something new. I am surprised how many classrooms don't allow children to try a new activity or apply new learning more than once or twice. I am surprised how many of us don't give ourselves that opportunity in our classrooms either! Very likely the first few times you teach writing in your classroom in a new way, your students will not write well. You need to show them how and give them many, many opportunities to practice these valuable new skills. Don't expect perfection the first time; writing doesn't work that way. Writing gets better by keeping a sharp eye on form, strategies, organization, and voice over time (Murray 2004). Your teaching of writing will get better, too.

Maintain an Active Classroom

When students are active, they are involved in their learning—they are naturally engaged. When you move about the room, you make yourself available and open to interact with your students.

If you're being honest, you may not think of student activity as a desired state. I know the feeling. When I was teaching kindergarten, I would wake up in the middle of the night in a cold sweat from a recurring nightmare in which thirty-two children were running around the room, climbing on chairs, and throwing magnetic letters at one another. (I worked very hard to ensure that nightmare never came true!) But *active* doesn't mean out of control. A well-designed and well-managed classroom is a classroom filled with active children: they know their limits and have been taught appropriate and proper ways to find a writing spot, get a piece of writing paper, use the interactive word wall, and share their writing with a friend.

Active learners move about the room physically; they are not required to sit in one desk or chair all day long. This is very important for young children. They need to move their physical muscles to keep their thinking muscles working—to keep their brains activated and focused on the task at hand.

Active learners move about mentally as well (Berninger and Winn 2006). Engaged children are partners in learning; they don't sit and passively listen to the teacher as she pours forth information they are to remember and retain. Engaged children interact with the new learning, the task at hand, the process to complete (Hidi and Boscolo 2006). The teacher learns from the children as they learn from her, from the interaction, and from one another. Children move about the room mentally by focusing on the teacher, on their writing, on the writing charts hanging around the room, on a word wall in a corner, on a peer, or perhaps on a book in the classroom library. They transport themselves to a "learning place"—a state of "mental flow" in which learning comes naturally, where time seems suspended while they engage deeply in an activity or an idea (Csikszentmihalyi 1990). This sense of effortless flow helps children feel good about writing and builds their belief in themselves and their ability to write. The more the children believe they have something to say and are able to say it, the more interested they will be in writing and, therefore, the more they will write (Hidi and Boscolo 2006).

Create Opportunities for Talking and Thinking

Good teaching is student centered. The writing workshop is student-centered learning. Minilessons focus on what students need to learn and take into consideration *how* children learn (Perry, Turner, and Meyer 2006). Children are then allowed to choose what to write and are supported while doing so.

Student-centered learning engages children because it is paired with student-centered teaching (Berninger and Winn 2006). When children are at the center of your teaching, you slow down and ensure they are learning. By that I don't mean you stop or get lazy—quite the opposite! You teach at the speed of learning, which means you reteach, support, scaffold, and model. You don't rush; you push (gently) to ensure children are learning and stop at nothing to make sure *they get it*. When you teach at the speed of learning, standards are living, vibrant learning objectives rather than a stale checklist in a teaching manual. Standards become visible occurrences, tangible actions. What will children do and say when they have learned a standard; what kind of writing will they produce?

Teach your objectives based on your vision of what the children will be doing and saying. Here's an example. A national standard for topic development is students will ". . . generate their own topics and spend the necessary amount of time to revisit and refine their writing" (August and Vockley 2002, 173). Picture a child doing this. What is he saying? What is he doing? I see a child working at his desk with his writing folder open. On his left is a paper that lists several writing topics he brainstormed a couple of days ago. He has circled one of those topics in green crayon and has also written it across the top of the piece of writing paper that is slightly askew in front of him. He is tapping his pencil on his bottom lip and glancing at the ceiling—thinking to himself. He looks back down and writes several lines, then looks at the word wall across the room. He finds the word he is searching for and copies it on his page. He blurts out to another student writing at the same table, "Hey, look, I wrote three lines! I am writing about my dog."

I could go on, but the point is, when you read standards and write learning objectives, *imagine what students should be doing*. Then you can ensure that you provide scaffolds to help them think and talk about their writing.

Good writers also engage in writing habits and processes. They write regularly, generate topics in which they are interested, and express themselves with energy and passion. They know that writing is fun, is sometimes hard, but is worthwhile—real work that is shared in a community (New Standards Primary Literacy Committee 1999). Here are some of the things children are involved in during writing workshop (Graves 2003; Murray 2004):

- visioning
- revisioning
- thinking like writers
- talking about thinking

Children have to talk through their writing to help them focus; talking helps young writers think and encourages them to internalize their stories long enough to transcribe them onto the page. Remember, young children have to think hard to put their thoughts into words; this skill is not yet automatic. Talk helps children remember their brainstorm, helps them keep it in short-term memory so they can simultaneously remember what they were thinking, the words they know how to spell, how to stretch out the sounds in words they don't know how to spell, and which sounds connect to which letters.

Talk develops vocabulary. Children who write need to develop a *composing vocabulary*—words to use when they talk about their writing, the writing process, and genre (Pritchard and Honeycutt 2006). When children are planning and drafting, they talk and listen to one another's ideas. When they are revising, they use words specific to revision. When editing and publishing, they focus on getting things just right—their talking, thinking, and listening now include words at this microlevel.

Hearing and seeing a word isn't enough for children to own the word—to be able to generate the word on their own, to recall it from memory and use it in talk or writing at will, without a prompt (Stahl and Nagy 2006; Stahl 1999). On the other hand, hearing and seeing words do develop children's *comprehension* of those words—that is, they understand a word's meaning when they hear it used in a sentence or read it (Marzano 2004; Stahl 1999). You want children both to comprehend words and to generate them on their own.

Children need to talk and think like writers. When children talk like writers, they might discuss

■ the organization of their piece
■ how to hook a reader
■ how their piece engages readers
■ where they use beautiful language
■ the type of details that make their writing come alive

When children think like writers, they may notice

■ word choice in a passage, poem, or favorite book
■ how an author uses beautiful language to engage and entertain
■ the way a book begins
■ how illustrations illuminate words
■ techniques writers use, like description and dialogue
■ how an author has organized her piece

By talking and thinking like writers, children go beyond hearing or reading a book or poem or nonfiction piece only for enjoyment; they use the text to learn how to write. The model piece of writing can have been created by one of their classmates, be the work of a published author, or be pulled from a Web-based resource.

When children talk, they engage. They don't sit passively; they learn through interaction. They are involved. They are thinking. They are learning language as well as learning to write. Good teaching provides the opportunity for this talking and thinking to come together to create that invisible but almost tangible space between teacher and students in which learning occurs.

Teaching with Energy

Thinking is critical for learning and writing, as are energy and engagement and interaction. However, you also have to focus your energy into that invisible learning space and create a moment of expectancy. Children expect you to show them *how* and then give them the chance to practice. If your energy is low, you lower the electric current pulsating through that learning space. This isn't just physical energy but emotional energy. Your body language and what you say and do tell children how you feel about what—and whom—you are teaching. Focus and center your energy. Keep your emotional energy as high as you can. If you do, you will delight in your students' learning and writing, and they will too.

CHAPTER TWO

Writing Workshop

The Essential Components

Leila snuggled up beside me with her writing folder in her lap. "Listen to me, please?" Her big eyes looked directly into mine. I nodded, and Leila began. She placed her finger deliberately and carefully under each word she had written, pausing once in a while to look carefully at a word and remember what she had written.

"Excellent!" I clapped my hands and got up, thanking her enthusiastically for reading her piece to me. I turned to leave the classroom but stopped for one more look. The children were so young yet so focused on their writing. I could feel the air in the room lifting up each child, pulling each to learn, to believe, to write. I felt the air lifting me up, too. I didn't want to leave. I returned to the center of the classroom and listened to another child read his piece. His finger slid unsteadily beneath each word as he read his big, scrawling first-grade print aloud to me.

Kristina, the teacher, who had been conferring with two children, walked by and asked, "So what do you think of our narratives?"

"Fabulous, simply fabulous," I said. I knew how much work it took to teach these twenty first graders to understand the genre and to give them the stamina to write well each day. Kristina made it look easy; she didn't even break a sweat. Her workshop flowed well.

Why Writing Workshop?

You need to teach writing and your students need to write. Writing workshop is a structure, a model, for doing so. Writing workshop nurtures writers. It gives them time to practice; it shows them how to navigate the writing process. Most important, it gives you a framework within which to work. When you implement writing workshop, you have explicit criteria to guide you. And it is simple. In a workshop, you teach short, powerful lessons and children write.

As I work with teachers across the nation on how to help children read and write well, I am often asked why I believe so strongly in workshop teaching. What I really believe in is the structure of the workshop. Instruction is best when it is brief and gives children time to think about and process what they've learned. Instruction is best when followed immediately by student engagement—a time to practice, to write.

For me, the classroom is a creative place in which children come together to learn, process that learning, talk, and guide one another. This type of learning doesn't occur unless children are allowed to talk to, work with, and bounce ideas off one another. A silent, restrictive classroom might seem like going back to basics, but it doesn't prepare students for the contemporary workplace, where people provide customer service or solve problems in teams (Flores, Cousin, and Diaz 1991).

As teachers, we have to work and talk and think together to learn how to serve our students well. No longer can we each go into our room and close our door, manage our own little factory. Collaboration is now the gold standard, and the workshop is just the place for all of us (teacher and student) to work and learn together. Our work as teachers is to apprentice children's thinking and ability to write (Boscolo and Gelati 2007). We teach them by taking their hands, gradually showing them *how* until they can do it on their own.

Most important, when we apprentice children's learning, we help struggling writers access language, writing, and thinking. Struggling writers need additional help in order to know and understand how to write, which includes how to get words on the page, how to record their ideas and thinking, and how to write in a particular genre. Children who struggle need extra support and scaffolds in order to own the writing process and control their ability to write the words that express their ideas and thinking. The workshop is the perfect place to nurture and guide their abilities.

The Workshop as Lesson Design

Two important elements of the writing workshop are

1. student engagement (see Chapter 1)
2. short, precise instruction (see Chapter 4)

I would love to be able to say, "Just do it. Just teach writing," and jump in, describing rich and powerful minilessons, sharing inspiring and moving student writing, and showing you how your classroom can become a beautiful, language-rich resource for your students. But over time I've learned this approach isn't particularly helpful. The helpful way to begin is to address your concerns, the biggest usually being *How?*

Recently I met with a group of primary teachers who were considering how to implement writing instruction at their school. "There is no way I can teach writing in a workshop!" one teacher exclaimed. "My principal won't allow it. She expects us to use the textbook and only the textbook."

Another teacher at the table said, "Yeah, I want kids to write, but I just can't do it. I feel too overwhelmed. And why do we have to teach writing so completely anyway? The kids aren't tested on writing for another two years."

The lead third-grade teacher agreed. "I just don't have time. I have to spend two and half hours teaching reading! When will I possibly teach writing? And I don't want another program. I am exhausted from programs."

These teachers were telling me the truth. They were teaching in a school designated as needing improvement by the accountability systems set up in No Child Left Behind legislation. They were tired of working so hard to pull students further than they had been taken before, negotiate time constraints, and prove to their principal that their students were learning.

I took a deep breath. These teachers were telling me something I have heard many times before when I've introduced the idea of writing workshop. Adding yet one more element to the school day is just too much. I began tentatively, not wanting to frustrate the group more than they already were. "I am here because your principal invited me. It truly is possible to teach writing in your compact day without using another program. You just have to want it, want your students to write well, with passion and ability."

"Oh, I want it," declared the lead third-grade teacher. "I just don't believe it is possible."

"Well," I said, "let's begin by focusing on the lesson design within the workshop. That's what your principal is looking for; that's what the team of consultants who are coaching your school on how to improve is looking for; that's what your kids are looking for, too. Stability. Focus. Routine."

The writing workshop is a structure for teaching writing. It isn't a writing program; it's a writing model. A writing model shows you how to teach children to write and gives them the time and space to do so. A program gives you a teacher's manual and activities for skills practice. There is nothing wrong with adopting a writing program, but it works best when applied within a writing model. Writing workshop is such a model. It is lesson design. It's the way teaching and learning unfold during the time designated in your schedule for teaching writing.

When some teachers I work with hear the term *lesson design*, they think of Madeline Hunter's lesson design (Saphier, Haley-Speca, and Gowen 2008; Perry, Turner, and Meyer 2006). Others think lesson design is related to the backward mapping developed by Wiggins and McTighe (1998). It's really a little bit of both, plus more.

Overall, you have to know the structure of your workshop, and you have to know where you are going. To know where you are going, you need to work backward from what your classroom curriculum, specifically your writing instruction, needs to accomplish. In structuring your workshop, you should include the best parts of Hunter's lesson planning model—explicitly show students how to express themselves in writing and use strategies to learn and remember to write well (Pressley and Harris 2006). Show students how, then give them time to work, to practice their new learning.

But workshop lesson design goes beyond both these structures. A workshop is based on the participatory model of learning. Children construct knowledge because they are active and participate in the process and the lessons. When children construct knowledge about writing and learn strategies to apply to the writing process, they learn to be writers (Schraw 2006; Harris and Graham 1996). You teach the writer, not the writing. Workshop instruction guides learning and assumes that children will learn when you

- show and tell them explicitly how to do something
- give them ample time to practice and explore
- compare and contrast their writing with their peers' and published authors' writing
- establish a rubric based on generally accepted writing standards
- joyfully celebrate their exploration of ideas, information, and print

The Writing Workshop as Instructional Model

Strategy instruction helps children become writers—and become better writers—by teaching the elements of writing: developing ideas, writing a draft, and revising that draft (Graham 2006b). Children need the time and the freedom to discover the incredible joy and self-confidence that comes from sharing their thoughts and words with the world (Spandel 2005). Often children who are struggling writers spend too little time *writing* and spend a lot of time doing writing exercises. Children who need help to write need time to write each day. By writing, they build self-confidence and find success. This is the goal of the writing workshop.

Writing workshop focuses on the specific processes of planning and idea development, drafting and revision, editing, and publication, teaching strategies within these processes so children become successful writers— and *feel* successful. They come to *own* these strategies, which means they are conscious of the choices that help them write (Cunningham and Cunningham 2002; Harris and Graham 1996). To that end, children must also own the workshop. They should set their own goals, generate ideas for their writing, produce writing, and reread and evaluate their writing (and the writing of others). When they do these things, their writing abilities will improve (Rijlaarsdam and van den Bergh 2006).

Remember, a workshop is a model, not a program: it is a flexible framework on which you hang your teaching. Setting up a workshop isn't hard. You may just need to conceptualize your classroom space a little differently:

- If your students' desks are in rows, move them into clusters so that children can share their writing easily or talk about how a book inspires their own writing.
- Create a space for teaching and learning (see Figures 2.1 and 2.2). This meeting area can do double duty as a work area for wiggly writers as well.
- Create areas in which to store books of many types and genres that will entice and energize young writers.
- Designate wall space on which to hang important charts created during the minilessons (see Figure 2.3).
- Set up a place for storing various papers, pencils, pens, and markers. These are the key equipment young children need to write (see Figure 2.4).

FIGURE 2.1 The Classroom Meeting Area Is a Space for Communal Learning

FIGURE 2.2 Great Meeting Areas Expose Children to Books and Are Print Rich

FIGURE 2.3 This Third-Grade Classroom Is Filled With Charts That Help Students Learn

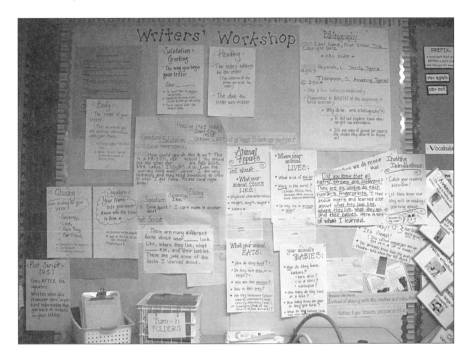

FIGURE 2.4 Writing Materials Organized in a Writing Center

- Create a system for storing and accessing writing folders. This can be as simple as a crate or bucket next to tables or desk clusters (see Figure 2.5), or it can include procedures for passing out, filing, and removing written work.
- Set up an organized space for the teaching materials you'll need during the workshop—pens, markers, sticky notes, paper (see Figures 2.6 and 2.7).

Learning, understanding, and harnessing the power of the writing workshop allows you to teach with urgency, to feel the passion you need to ensure you are giving your students what they need to know, when they need to know it, with purpose and focus. If you feel this urgency to ensure that all the children in your classroom learn to write well, they will. Complicated structures make feeling this urgency and teaching to it difficult. With a complicated structure you end up focusing on too many other things, when all you really need to focus on is the children.

The workshop structure allows you to teach; it allows children to write. This sounds simple, but it can be more complicated than you might imagine. Focusing on teaching means that you are making new learning

- relevant to children
- accessible
- understandable
- visible
- easy

FIGURE 2.5 Students' Writing Folders Are Stored Next to Their Desks

Chapter Two

FIGURE 2.6   This Teaching Area Allows Easy Access to Materials

FIGURE 2.7   Teaching Materials Organized in Bins

FIGURE 2.8   Elements of the Writing Workshop

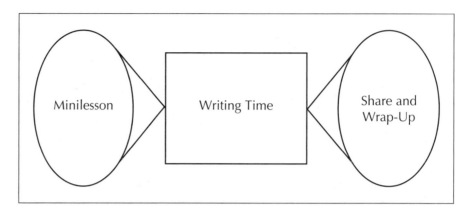

The simpler the framework within which you work, the easier it is to teach. The writing workshop framework includes three sections (see Figure 2.8):

- minilesson
- shared, guided, and/or independent writing
- share and wrap-up

Starting It Off: A Well-Designed Minilesson

The minilesson is the power source of your workshop. It is the engine that drives motivation and learning. The minilesson focuses on the children and what you want them to learn. As you work to meet learning expectations, a well-designed minilesson carefully guides students' attention, engagement, and focus as well as their ability to take in and remember new ideas and information (Pritchard and Honeycutt 2006). The minilesson is short, lasting between five and fifteen minutes. In a minilesson you provide explicit, direct instruction focused on *one* objective—and *only* one. You model, examine, explain, show, think, and demonstrate. (You don't lecture, which is telling without showing how.) First you plan what strategy you are going to teach and how you are going to teach it. Then you help children learn the strategy so that they can successfully apply it independently (Graham and Harris 2007). (Chapter 4 explains minilessons in more depth.)

Putting It Into Practice: Writing, Writing, Writing

The writing time is the transformative heart of the workshop. After presenting the minilesson, you enthusiastically tell your students, "Try it!" The children settle in their writing spots and begin the hard but exciting work of putting their ideas on paper. During this independent writing, children think about what they want to share with the world and what words to put on paper in order to do so. Every time they write, children experience the wonder of discovery, the satisfaction of connecting with others. You might ask very young children to participate in shared and guided writing. Older students (those in second and third grade) should be writing pieces several pages long, in specific genres. (Chapter 5 discusses the writing portion of the workshop in more depth.)

Bringing It Together: Share and Wrap-Up

After the children write, you don't just rush on to the next item on your daily agenda. Rather, you carefully and deliberately bring the students together to celebrate what they've accomplished. You highlight what the children have attempted and successfully achieved, validate and reinforce the important skill or concept they have learned, and reteach your objective one more time.

As the children share their thinking and their writing, you remind them one more time what you taught them. You celebrate children's learning and then remind them how it is like (or perhaps unlike) the minilesson. Helping them see their work in light of their new learning gives you a chance to reiterate and reinforce important points. Children need to reflect on new learning several times before it sinks in. This is also your chance to assess your class and think about how you might want to tweak the next day's minilesson.

Ideally, when you teach using the workshop structure, everyone is having fun, the students are easily engaged, and learning is relevant. These ideals are achieved because your teaching is rich, relevant, and focused on your students. The seven essential elements of reading workshop I discuss in *Teaching Reading in a Title I School, K–3* (2008) also apply to writing workshop:

- You explicitly describe the strategy.
- You provide direct instruction, and the students try, or practice, the strategy.
- You model the strategy or skill.
- You gradually release responsibility to the students.
- Students model and teach strategies and skills for and to one another.
- Independent practice is relevant and focused on the students.
- Students are immersed in a print-rich environment.

CHAPTER THREE

Teaching Charts
Visual Scaffolds for Young Children, English Learners, and Reluctant Writers

Teaching charts are must-have tools for bringing learning to life. If you use teaching charts in your minilessons, visual learners will be engaged and supported, and all students will have a record of teaching and learning they can consult to help them be responsible for their learning and remember *how* to write.

Teaching charts help us scaffold learning for struggling writers. When you are adapting your instruction to include more support to ensure that children who don't know and understand *learn* to know and understand, think carefully about moving from mostly oral presentations to a mix of oral and visual presentations during your minilessons. By making the teaching point clear through a teaching chart, by highlighting language and preserving ideas in print, you not only scaffold children's learning and thinking during the lesson and the workshop but also create a learning record that you can refer to over and over again to connect learning, new thinking, and ideas for struggling writers.

There is a difference between saying, showing and saying, and showing and writing down for further reference:

- *Saying and showing*: "When you are writing today, I want you to add details to bring your characters alive. I am going to add details to the second and third sentences of the story I began about the time my little sister ruined my birthday cake. Watch as I add a caret and write in the additional words." *The students hear the teacher say what he is going to do and then watch him do it.*

Notice the difference when the teacher records what he is saying:

- *Saying, showing, and writing down*: "When you are writing today, I want you to add details to bring your characters alive. Remember when we learned about character traits during reading workshop? [*Points to the character trait chart (Figure 3.1).*] Well, we are going to use this chart to help us with our writing. On the chart I wrote that details bring characters alive because they make their thinking and action more believable. Details include specific things the person did or something she said. So I could add actions and/or dialogue to my story about the time my sister ruined my birthday cake. I am going to add details about how she stuck her hand in the frosting. Watch while I do this." (The completed teaching chart is shown in Figure 3.2.) *The children hear what the teacher wants them to focus on, they watch him write the expectations on a chart, and they hear him think out loud about those expectations as he writes them down. They have time to think about the definition of adding details and the criteria for doing so. Then they watch their teacher add details to his writing.*

FIGURE 3.1   Character Trait Chart

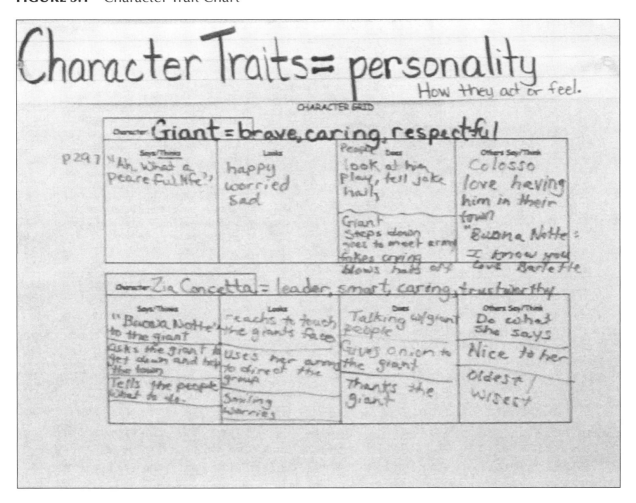

FIGURE 3.2 Teaching Chart on Bringing Characters Alive

How to Add Details to Your Writing to Bring Characters Alive

Add details to tell the reader specific things about

- *What someone did*

- *What someone said*

FOCUS on writing specific action!

My story about my sister:

Original Story:	Revised Story:
My sister makes me mad. I made a birthday cake for my 18th birthday. It was all finished and on the counter. When I wasn't home, my sister cut a piece for her and her friends, but she didn't tell me. At night, I found out the cake was ruined!	My sister makes me mad. I made a birthday cake for my 18th birthday. I put pink roses and yellow curls on the cake. I left it on the counter in the kitchen. I went out and when I wasn't home, my sister came home with her friends. She knew that was my birthday cake, but she ate it anyway. She cut a piece for her and her friends, but she didn't tell me. After dinner, my mom went to get the cake. I wanted to put candles on it. She brought the cake out and ¼ of the cake was gone. I found out the cake was ruined! I told her, "I am so mad at you. You at the cake!" She laughed really loudly, and then said, "I'm sorry!"

Teaching Charts as Effective Learning Tools

I encourage an abundant use of teaching charts; you cannot have too many. These indelible records of learning and teaching help students remain engaged when they are working on their own. They can reread and refer to a chart (see the examples in Figures 3.3 and 3.4) to help themselves write; they don't need you beside them 100 percent of the time telling them what to do. You *teach*, *show*, *model*, and *record* while creating the chart and then remind students to refer to the chart (the record of the teaching) to help themselves. You are right there to redirect or reteach as necessary, but their own thinking, prompted by the chart, is their first course of action when they get confused.

FIGURE 3.3 Teaching Chart Listing Strategies for Writing Nonfiction

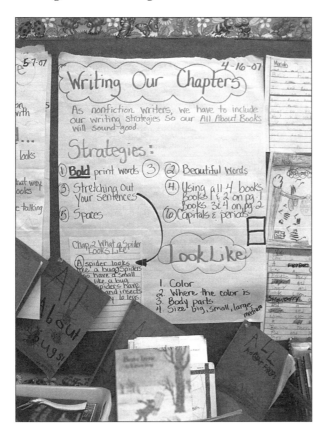

FIGURE 3.4 Teaching Chart Emphasizing Research for an All-About Book

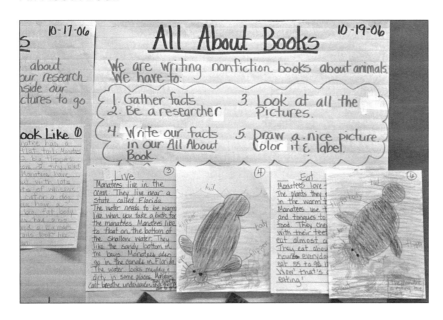

A teaching chart helps children become apprentices in the classroom (Pressley et al. 2007; Englert, Mariage, and Dunsmore 2006). Children who rely solely on the teacher spend a lot of time sitting and waiting. If you create clear charts, the children will be able to think for themselves as they work independently; you'll strengthen their thinking muscles and ensure that they are engaged in the work of the classroom and trying things on their own. You'll also be able to see what they understand and whether they are beginning to own information.

Teaching charts help you

- show students what to do
- capture in writing what you're doing while thinking aloud
- create a record that you and the children can refer to over and over again

As stimuli to learning, teaching charts

- reinforce paths of learning and memory in the brain
- reinforce the three levels of knowing: association, comprehension, and generation
- help you gradually release responsibility for learning to your students
- document the thinking process
- outline steps and break learning into chunks
- connect visually with students—different fonts (large, small, italicized, bold), different colors, various text features (headings, lists, bullets)

As archives of discussions, lessons, and thinking, teaching charts

- remind children of past learning
- help visual and kinesthetic learners (they can see and touch the charts)
- teach research skills (children need to locate information on the chart)
- teach language (children link words and phrases with related pictures or graphics)

As focal points during instruction, charts

- direct student focus and attention during the minilesson
- help students think
- help students maintain their line of thinking while they listen to and watch you teach

Teaching Charts Ensure Student Involvement

Teaching charts engage learners (an emotional connection) because they involve them in the lesson (a physical or mental action) (Fletcher 2008). When you are active, you start to feel a connection to what you are doing (Boscolo and Gelati 2007; Englert, Mariage, and Dunsmore 2006; McCutchen 2006). You have to involve students in the minilesson before they are able to benefit from the autonomy of working on their own. Student involvement is a much deeper concept than physical motion or some other form of participation in the minilesson, followed by making decisions about what to write (Perry, Turner, and Meyer 2006). Involvement includes

- allowing and encouraging high levels of student authority: giving students the opportunity to say what they feel, validating their ideas, and giving them permission to act on their thoughts and feelings while writing (Fletcher 2008)
- using interrelated strategies (teaching charts and pair shares, for example) in every lesson to ensure all students are learning
- explicitly showing students how to use a strategy to help them become self-regulated learners (Graham and Harris 1996)
- providing sustainable structures of support (Fletcher 2008): using dependable and routine minilesson structures so children won't worry about what they are supposed to do and how to do it

Teaching Charts Increase Comprehension and Vocabulary

Charting lessons promotes students' ability to articulate their thoughts and comprehend what they hear; it also increases their vocabulary. *Comprehension* is generally defined as the ability to understand and recall what one has heard or read (Biemiller 1999). Often teachers think of comprehension only in relation to reading instruction, but it is essential to everything that happens in the classroom. When we talk to children, tell them information, read aloud to them, or share our ideas with them, they have to listen to—and understand—what we say. This skill is often taken for granted, but children increase their vocabulary and improve their comprehension as much through class discussions and teacher presentations than by reading (Biemiller 1999).

The act of making a chart during a lesson makes you slow your teaching down and be explicit. It ensures you are teaching at the speed of your students' memory and level of development. It helps children comprehend what you are teaching them (Sinatra et al. 1998). By being specific, you help children visualize what they are going to learn. You also contextualize your instruction for English learners, who need the language they hear to be understandable and put into context (Gibbons 2002). Writing ideas and information on a chart contextualizes language for children and helps them focus on what is being said, instead of feeling lost in a stream of language that doesn't make sense.

The chart in Figure 3.5 captures the idea of helping children with topic development in nonfiction writing and shows children a way of thinking about a topic. Shana created this chart while teaching her first graders about how to choose an animal to write about for a report. She slowed her thinking down and said everything aloud as she thought it so the children could experience how her inner voice went about brainstorming topics. First she brainstormed a list with the children of what animals they had been learning about, and then she showed the children a technique of using their hand to identify five facts to ensure they knew enough about their topic. She then demonstrated how she focused her topic by writing it on a sticky note. Figure 3.6 is a chart a third-grade teacher created to show her students how to generate ideas for writing by focusing on emotions.

FIGURE 3.5 Nonfiction Topic Development Chart

FIGURE 3.6 Another Chart That Helps Children Brainstorm Writing Topics

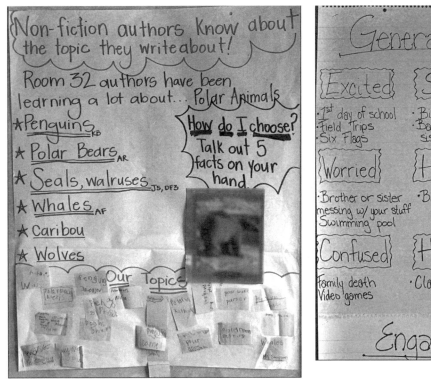

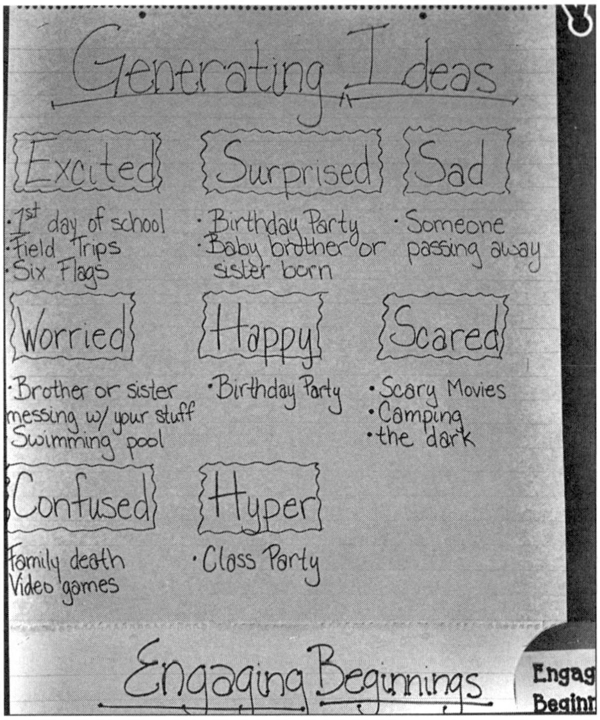

FIGURE 3.7 Academic Vocabulary Identifying the Steps in Writing a Letter

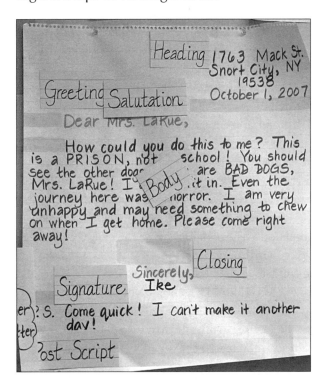

Biemiller's (1999) research on vocabulary development reveals that a child scoring 25 percent on standardized vocabulary tests at age three has, at age twelve in sixth grade, the listening vocabulary of an average eight-year-old third grader. Anything we do to accelerate the listening and comprehension vocabulary of children in our classrooms will increase their ability to hear and understand. By adding academic vocabulary to our teaching charts (see the examples in Figures 3.7, 3.8, and 3.9); repeating these words often during our minilessons; and expecting students to use these words in class discussions, while writing independently, and during sharing sessions, we increase our students' vocabularies (Nagy 1988).

Why Use Teaching Charts?

Teaching charts serve many purposes: they engage students, ensure that your instruction is direct and broken into small, manageable steps, develop students' listening comprehension skills, and are powerful independent learning resources children can turn to again and again, whatever the genre. Teaching charts also increase English learner's chances to learn academic language—terms like *summarizing*, *analyzing*, *evaluating*, and *comparing*, for example (Dutro and Moran 2003).

Some teachers view these powerful teaching tools with suspicion. Perhaps they find the thought of creating charts overwhelming or worry that they won't be artistic enough or that the walls will look cluttered. But your charts don't have to be beautiful, just purposeful. And you can guard against overkill: display only the ones that help children learn.

I encourage you to buy a big tablet of paper and some markers. Remember that as responsive educators, we need to use what works, whether we are entirely comfortable with the technique or not. Jump in! With time and a bit of practice, it will become easier.

When you create a chart in front of children, they become part of the action and the experience. While you teach, model, talk, and write, they are thinking about information they know and remembering past experiences. The hope is that they will feel validated, energized, and affirmed, rather than confused. Even if they are a bit confused initially, they may feel an aha connection when the confusion lifts and they understand. The emotions students feel while we are creating the chart with them helps them remember (Jensen 2000).

It's important to leave the chart as is—don't be tempted to rewrite it after school so it will be perfect or beautiful. Even if there are spelling or thinking mistakes on the chart, don't change a thing! Modeling your fix-up strategies when you make a mistake is a powerful teaching moment: children learn how to handle their own mistakes, another emotional connection. When that chart hangs in the room for children to glance at over and over again throughout the day, they are reminded of the writing point taught as well as all of the other learning that occurred while the chart was being made.

FIGURE 3.8 A Synonym Chart

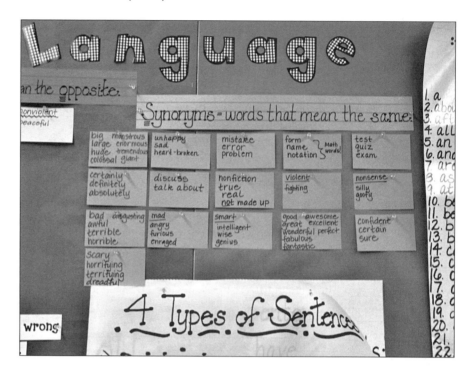

FIGURE 3.9 A Chart Introducing a Label for a Writing Technique

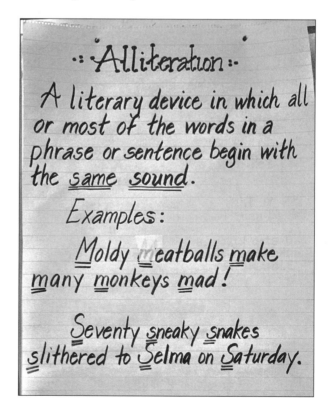

Chapter Three

Using Interactive Whiteboards

Recently educators have started using interactive whiteboards, known as Smart Boards, as a teaching tool. Interactive whiteboards have the power to engage students during a lesson or group practice. But unless you're careful, you can get caught up in using the technology and forget to focus on learning.

When using interactive whiteboards, first note the purpose and goal of your lesson. These boards engage students best when you are teaching the lesson and have all eyes on you. You can display information, have students come up and add information, and move information around. But there are some issues to be aware of.

Focus on Engaging All Students

Unless students engage with this technology in new and powerful ways, interactive whiteboards reinforce learning patterns that are not considered best practice. The traditional teaching approach in which the teacher asks a question, a number of students raise their hands, one student answers, and the teacher confirms or disconfirms the answer keeps the teacher in control of the learning; she is the holder of knowledge, and the majority of students do not take part in the interaction. When one child comes up to the interactive whiteboard and writes an answer, you are engaging only one student at a time while the rest watch. You want to engage all of the brains in the room at the same time, not just one. Some ways to do that are presented in Figure 3.10.

The point of a minilesson (see Chapter 4) is to directly and explicitly teach a writing objective in a short burst of instruction that all your students can relate to, participate in, and remember. You can do all of these things while using an interactive whiteboard; just approach your instruction in new ways:

- Instead of having one student answer at a time, have students work in pairs or groups and have a representative come up and share a group answer.
- Instead of directing a question to a particular group, ask all groups to think through the question and formulate an answer; then call one group up to work with the interactive whiteboard.
- Instead of confirming or correcting a group's answer yourself, lead a discussion in which all the groups decide whether the answer is correct and revise it if they think it isn't.

Create a Permanent Chart to Display in the Room

Technology is wonderful, but the images displayed on an interactive whiteboard are fleeting. The information disappears when it is not on the screen. When we move on to the next thing, the chart is no longer there to point to while we connect the information captured on it with other information. Students can't glance at it at other times during the day.

FIGURE 3.10 Ways to Strategically Engage *All* Students

Use Questions to Engage

Ask children responding versus assessing questions:

1. Why did you choose to . . . ? Tell a partner.
2. How might your writing have changed if you had . . . ?
3. How does this part of your writing relate to your beginning, or ending, or middle?
4. I want to know more. What else happened?

Ask children to respond to each other:

1. Are there works you didn't know how to write?
2. What did you see in your mind while writing?
3. What part of my writing did you like best?
4. What did you see in your mind when I read my piece to you?

Ask children self-evaluation questions:

1. What part of your piece could be improved?
2. What is your favorite part of your piece?
3. Did you write all the details you see in your mind?
4. Did you focus on a memory moment?

Use Tools to Engage

Fist to Five

Have students use the fingers on one hand as a scale, showing a fist as the lowest ranking (zero) and all five fingers as the highest. Use fist to five to

- Ask children to analyze writing and compare it with teaching points or teaching charts—they rate if the writing models the teaching point or strategy
- Rate self-monitoring abilities:
  - I understand this well and can do it on my own.
  - I know this and can explain it to my writing partner.
  - I need help.
  - I need more practice.

Speedometer Writing

Think of a speedometer with 0 as the takeoff and speeding at 100. Have the student lay one arm on top of the other with hands touching elbows. Then the student can raise the top arm from 0 mph to 100 mph to show understanding.

Use for the same metacognitive and reflective thinking as in the fist-to-five activities.

Make sure to honor the emotional investment your students make when they help you create an electronic teaching chart by finding a way to redisplay it after you've clicked Close on the computer screen. Students need to be able to control when and how they reinforce their learning. It's important to find a way to put information stored in the computer on the walls of the classroom:

- Create a manual version of the chart at the same time students create it on the interactive whiteboard.
- Start out by creating a paper chart, then use the interactive whiteboard to extend the learning.
- Work through a minilesson on an interactive whiteboard; the next day create a paper chart to reinforce the learning.
- Save and print the computer image of the teaching chart; then, using poster-making software, create an enlarged version and hang it up in the classroom.
- Save and print the computer image of the teaching chart, make photocopies, and have each student place a copy in her writing resource binder or folder.

Creating Effective Teaching Charts

Of course no chart is perfect, but there are techniques to help you make them as effective as possible. Charts need to be carefully organized; they need to match the flow of the lesson, make it easy to retrieve the information they contain, and include features that capture and direct students' attention.

Remember that the charts you display connect your students to *you*. They build community. When I walk into a classroom filled with teaching charts, I see the personality of the teacher reflected on the walls. Your handwriting doesn't have to be perfect, and you don't have to be an artist. You just need to represent learning on your walls in a way that lets your students connect to you and deepen and reinforce their own learning. The effect is priceless.

It's best to have the basics in place before you start: the title, definitions (if any), illustrations that would be hard to draw while teaching. Preparation like this usually takes just two or three minutes.

A good way to differentiate and direct students' attention to information is to use color:

- Use a different color for each line of text.
- Make the title a different color from the body of the chart.
- Highlight vocabulary words in a different color.
- Highlight words that signal action (directions) in bold, dark colors.
- Underline, circle, or box words in a color different from that of the words themselves.

Other text features can be just as powerful. For example:

- Put words in boldface type.
- Italicize words.
- Draw pictures and sketches.
- Create headings.
- Code parts of the text with a symbol and put the key at the bottom or in a corner.
- Define terms or provide synonyms.
- Use bulleted or numbered lists.

Example Teaching Chart: "How Do You Spell . . . ? Using the Room Around You"

The teaching chart in Figure 3.11 was created during a minilesson on things students can do to help them spell common words. Notice how the chart attracts and directs students' attention. The title, in bold at the bottom, tells students what the chart is about. Putting the title at the bottom reduces any confusion that might be caused by the long bulleted list. The sentence at the top explicitly states what students can do to help them spell words: look in different places around the room. The chart then not only lists these places

FIGURE 3.11 Teaching Chart Prepared During a Spelling Minilesson

but includes a picture next to each bullet point to help young readers (and English learners) understand even if they don't know all the words. Look at all the effective features:

- a title at the bottom of page
- an umbrella heading telling students where to look for help
- a clear bulleted list with accompanying pictures
- bullet points consistently presented as prepositional phrases
- bright colors
- underlined words

Example Teaching Chart: "Does Your Story Tell It All?"

Charts can be created for various purposes: to define terms and vocabulary, outline directions for independent work, capture what you do as you model a process, highlight text features, or record information to build students' knowledge (about a particular genre, for example). The chart in Figure 3.12 focuses on telling a complete story. Young children often begin a story one day, run out of time, and assume they need to begin a new story the next day. This chart redirects children to *add on* to their writing, to begin to understand and control the conventions of narrative.

FIGURE 3.12 Teaching Chart on Expanding a Narrative

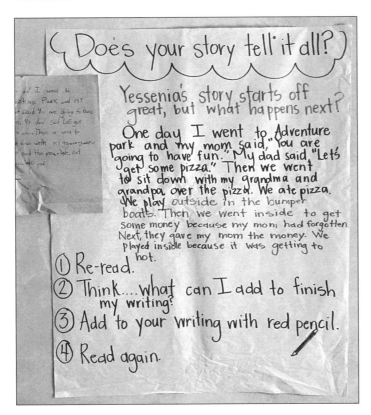

The title, at the top this time, has a circle drawn around it so children will clearly recognize that it is a title and not part of the directions. (Young children learning to read find a signal like this very helpful.) The chart then follows the design of the minilesson:

- It states the objective, which is to work on what happens next (adding on).
- It models how to add on (using a child's writing).
- It presents numbered steps on how to add on.

Again, look at the effective features this teacher has employed:

- The title is sectioned off.
- An example of student work is included, along with what the teacher thought aloud about it.
- Color differentiates the original writing from that which was added.
- Clear steps are listed for students to follow.

Example Teaching Charts from a Letter-Writing Unit

As children learn to write, they need clear and specific examples of what is expected of them. Kindergarten often includes a unit on letter writing. The chart in Figure 3.13, created during the first few minilessons of such a unit,

FIGURE 3.13 Teaching Chart Capturing the Basics of Letter Writing

FIGURE 3.14 Mrs. Blodgett's Model Letter

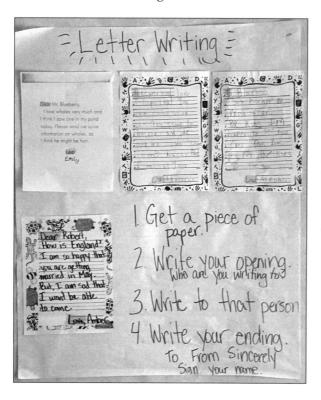

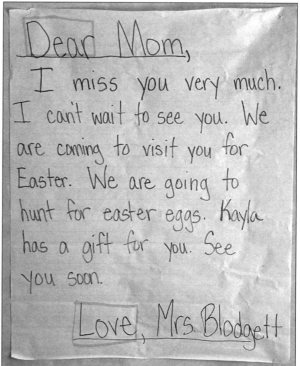

summarizes the basics. Titled simply "Letter Writing," it shows a letter from a favorite story the teacher has read aloud. It also shows two letters written by kindergartners in the class. The focus here is on introductions and endings, which in kindergarten is just *to* or *dear* at the beginning and *from* or *sincerely* at the end. The teacher also lists the steps she wants the children to follow during independent writing and places a model letter to the left of the steps. One glance at this chart lets you see the three elements of good instruction: *effective examples*, *explicit direction*, and *a model*.

After children learn what a letter is and how it is formatted, they are ready to write their own letters. The second chart from this unit, in Figure 3.14, is a model letter the teacher has created. During the minilesson she presented before the children wrote their letters, she went over the information from the chart in Figure 3.13 once again; then, on a large piece of paper, she modeled writing her letter, highlighting the salutation and complementary close with a yellow marker. It's smart to reuse charts in more than one minilesson, adding to the learning with a new example. Children retain information from familiar visuals. By using a chart a number of times, you reinforce new learning and create connections and patterns within the lessons. Young brains love patterns and connections. Structures like this help children remember and retrieve information.

The chart in Figure 3.15 extends the genre of letter writing beyond

FIGURE 3.15 Teaching Chart Modeling Things One Might Say in a Letter

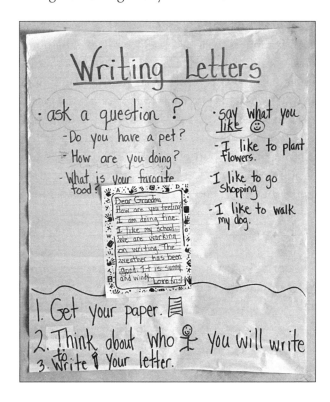

structure and discusses possible topics to write about. This chart was created during a minilesson Mrs. Blodgett presented after the children began to insist, "But I just don't know what to write in my letter!" The chart explores two possible subjects for letters—telling about things you like and asking questions. The left side of the chart models a few questions; the right side models statements about things one might like. The model includes both these subjects, questioning and sharing favorite things. At the bottom of the chart, Mrs. Blodgett again lists clear steps for the children to follow during independent writing, modeling the steps as she does so. She helped English learners know what to do by physically modeling each action after saying it and including basic illustrations.

In this series of lessons, Mrs. Blodgett carefully told the children what they were learning, showed them the steps in the process, shared examples and suggestions, and followed up by telling them everything again. Her charts supported her teaching and the students' learning.

Storing and Collecting Charts

At this point you may be thinking, *These charts look and sound great, but how would I store them all in my classroom?* There are easy ways to organize your charts so that you can use them again and again to teach and reteach. However, don't use the same charts from one year to the next—your students won't have an emotional connection to them unless they've helped create them. The point in making and using charts is to do it *with* your students.

Simple Storage

Use clip-type pant hangers to store related charts together for easy access. For longer-term storage, roll charts from a unit of study together and secure them with rubber bands. Don't forget to include an identifying label on the outside of the roll. Another approach is to tape two large pieces of corrugated cardboard together on one long side to create a hinge and then tape pieces of ribbon to the nonhinged sides, thus creating a portfolio. Place the charts from a unit inside the portfolio, tie the ribbons together, clearly label the top of the side that will face out, and store vertically with the hinge side down (like matted but unframed prints in an art gallery). You can store several portfolios together and flip through them easily.

Sophisticated Storage

Create a digital portfolio by photographing your favorite or most successful charts with a digital camera. Download the pictures onto your computer and use an online website to create a scrapbook of charts that work in your classroom. You can use this digital scrapbook to spark your creativity in planning lessons and remind you how you created charts in the past. You and your colleagues can share these files, learning from one another what works best in creating visuals for your students. Online scrapbooking sites include Shutterbug (www.shutterbug.com) and Kodak Gallery (www. kodakgallery.com).

You can also display digital photos of teaching charts on your Smart Board or project the images on a wall in your classroom with a computer and LCD projector. Second and third graders can easily access the digital portfolios on their own and look up information they might need to know if they are working in genres or using writing techniques you haven't reviewed in a while.

The Essentials

Remember the essentials of teaching charts:

- Identify one clear objective and set it off visually from the rest of the chart.
- Focus on one teaching point.
- Explain this teaching point in words, pictures, diagrams, art, and designs.
- Use color to delineate and highlight information.
- Use different fonts and sizes to showcase information.

PART 2

Teach

Nothing in our classrooms is more important than learning. Students who don't learn aren't going to live the same lives as children who do (blunt, but true).

We also need to make sure our students are learning the right stuff. To that end, we scour state standards documents to identify essential learning, flag effective writing lessons in our professional books, skim teaching manuals for powerful learning objectives, and use our school or district guidelines to help us focus on day-to-day curriculum—only to discover that even if we taught 24/7, we would never get to it all. (For more on developing standards, see my 2004 book *How to Align Literacy Instruction, Assessment, and Standards and Achieve Results You Never Dreamed Possible.*)

The most important thing we can do, after ensuring we are focused on the right things, is teach well. When we teach well, our students will know what to do and how to do it, will develop the skills, strategies, and conceptual knowledge they need to be successful writers. When we teach well we offer "cognitive apprenticeships" to our students (Cunningham and Cunningham 2002). We help them deepen their thinking and writing skills by telling, showing, modeling, and then letting go.

CHAPTER FOUR

The Minilesson
Ensuring Learning Through Explicit Instruction

The minilesson is the motivating force of the writing workshop; it prepares the way for children's writing and sharing work. Minilessons vary in focus and type. Some teach management skills, others teach writing skills and strategies, still others teach genre characteristics. The key to all minilessons is that they don't overload children with too much information before students are allowed to work with this information—*to go ahead and write.*

The Centerpiece of Writing Workshop

Why is the minilesson the centerpiece of the writing workshop? Isn't the children's writing most important? Or the books we read aloud to teach children how writing looks, sounds, and feels? Or the skills children practice? Quite frankly—and simply—no. Without the minilesson, writing workshop would be just another form of day care. (Although the children's writing runs a close second.)

The minilesson sets children free to write: to be brave, soulful, exploring, caring, and validating. These opportunities present themselves when children learn about writing. The lesson teaches the child, not the writing. Children come away with strategies that they try out and, by doing so, eventually *own.* Look at the strategies Justine has learned and uses in her piece about her hamster (see Figure 4.1). She writes with beautiful language (*quick as a wink*); she uses dialogue ("*Mama, Mama come here; my hamster is gone.*"); we see the situation unfold through the details. The piece stops abruptly when the hamster pops out of the toilet, but that's OK. Shana, Justine's wise and caring teacher, wants to teach Justine how to write; her goal is not to take a red pen and fix Justine's writing. Justine will learn to create satisfying endings in time, just as she has learned these other strategies.

Children who receive explicit instruction in genre characteristics and in writing habits, processes, strategies, and skills write better than children who do not receive explicit instruction (Donovan and Smolkin 2006; Graham and Harris 2007). Explicit instruction is a form of scaffolding (Chall

FIGURE 4.1   First Grader Justine's Narrative About Her Hamster

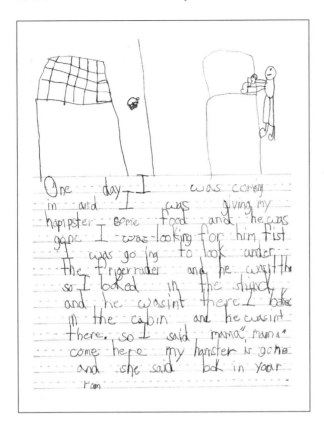

One day I was coming in and I was giving my hapister some food and he was gone. I was looking for him fist I was going to look under the tiger rader and he wasn't the so I looked in the stinck and he wasint there I loke in the cabin and he wasint there. so I said "mama", mama" come here my hamster is gone and she said bok in your ram

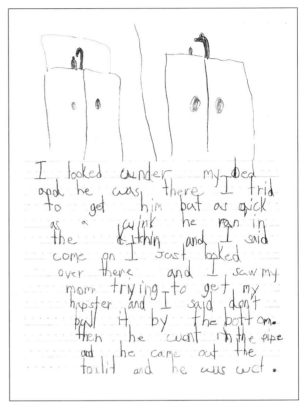

I looked under my bed and he was there. I trid to get him but as qick as a wink he ran in the thin and I said come on I just loked over there and I saw my mom trying to get my hapster and I said don't pol it by the bottom. then he want in the pipe and he came out the toilit and he was wet.

2000). In direct teaching, we model, tell, show, and demonstrate; we guide children along the path of learning. We break instruction into steps; we gently take children by the hand and show them: first this, then this, next that. The teaching chart in Figure 4.2 is an example of how to break instruction into explicit, purposeful steps—how to move children from where they are to where they need to be. Figure 4.3 is a teaching chart reminding children that readers need to be shown, not told, and giving an example of what showing, not telling, looks like.

Minilessons as Teaching Moments

Minilessons are just that: *mini*, or short. They are moments in which you explicitly and carefully tell children *how*. You begin a minilesson by waking up children's brains; after the neurons are firing, you unfold the lesson orally, visually, and kinesthetically, delivering a powerful learning punch in about ten minutes. (Minilessons can be as short as four or five minutes—perfect for reteaching and reviewing information—or as long as twenty minutes, but twenty minutes is the maximum attention span of pretty much *anyone*, so be careful.)

FIGURE 4.2 "We Are Good Writers Because . . ." Chart

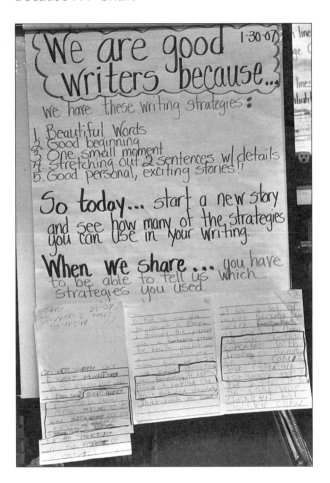

Minilessons are the antidote to too much teacher talk—lengthy lectures that don't engage students or help them own their learning. When children can no longer focus, they stop listening and start thinking about whatever tangential something has popped into their heads. However, too little teacher talk is also dangerous. If you don't tell your students *how* to do something new before you ask them to do it, you run the risk that the children will feel frustrated or just get things wrong (practice doesn't necessarily make perfect; it just makes permanent). Therefore, after showing children *how* in a minilesson, you then let them work on their own (with guidance, of course) to own the *how* for themselves.

Breaking the Minilesson Down Into Essentials

The four elements of a minilesson are

1. connecting with your students and "waking them up"
2. explicitly showing and telling them about a concept, strategy, or skill

FIGURE 4.3   Teaching Chart on Showing, Not Telling

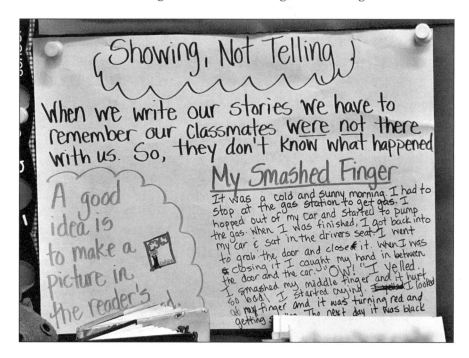

3. engaging them in thinking and talking about the concept, strategy, or skill

4. concluding the lesson and launching the writing session in which they apply the concept, strategy, or skill

Figure 4.4 (also included in the appendix as a reproducible) is a form that lets you lay out graphically the four things you must accomplish in a minilesson, allotting space to each in proportion to the time it takes. You'll do your heaviest lifting in your direct instruction as you artfully guide the children in their learning; there's enough room on the form for you to sketch a teaching chart in advance. You don't need to write out all your minilessons on this form; that would get tiresome and you are too busy. Use the form whenever you need help visualizing how you are going show and tell your students about the lesson objective and planning how children will think and talk about their learning. This learning tool can help you design more precise lessons and comes in very handy when you are developing units of study.

Components of Designing and Teaching a Minilesson

Preparation: Stating the Objective
The first thing you need to figure out is what you are teaching and what you want students to know how to do. Be clear. An unclear objective gets

FIGURE 4.4 Minilesson Plan

Minilesson Plan

Lesson Title _____ **Objective** _____

1. Connection	**2. Explicit Teaching** **(Show and Tell)**
3. Engagement	
4. Closure	

---

you off track, and if you are off track, your students will be, too. Here's an example of an unclear objective: _Students are going to brainstorm their favorite topics and "feelings" words and think about nonfiction structures for their next piece._ Reading this objective, I wonder, _What are the kids doing? Are these topics real events or imaginary ones? What are "feelings" words? Are they going to use a brainstormed topic to write a nonfiction narrative?_

When you write an objective, make sure it has a single, clear point. The way to be certain is to visualize your students doing what the objective says they will do. State it in ten words or less. This is hard to do but essential. We're a little afraid to say out loud what we are going to teach. What if we're wrong? What if we don't meet our expectations? Remember, it's OK to make mistakes. State the objective clearly in ten words or less; after you plan the minilesson, you can adjust the objective as necessary.

Begin like this: _At the end of the lesson, students will . . ._ Some possibilities include

- ■ . . . _generate a list of writing topics._ (six words)
- ■ . . . _focus on writing the relevant parts of a narrative._ (nine words)
- ■ . . . _add details to the middle of a previously written piece._ (ten words)
- ■ . . . _create an effective ending for a current narrative._ (eight words)

FIGURE 4.5 Teaching Chart Explaining How to Focus Writing with Details

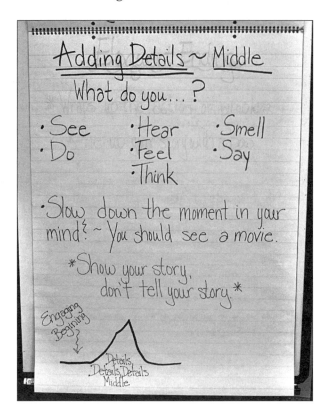

Let's pick the third one: *add details to the middle of a previously written piece.* How might we teach children to focus their use of details?

I would find examples of student writing that I found moving and thoughtful, read these out loud, and create a chart listing the differences of pieces with beautiful, moving details and pieces with a lack of focus and perhaps write some ideas of how to focus writing *small* on the chart as well. I would place a big basket of books in the middle of the meeting area and ask the children to look at the middle section of several books and discuss them with a partner. Finally, I would brainstorm ways authors add appropriate and effective details with the class and list them on a chart as well (see Figure 4.5). Concluding the minilesson, I would ask the children to think about the ways to focus their writing they talked about today and see whether they could add to or subtract details from (or write a better middle for) the pieces they were writing.

That's it. That's all I would do to introduce adding details. A little learning is more effective than dousing children with everything they need to know about a topic. I'd save some of the other things they needed to know for the next day's minilesson (and perhaps have them bring their pieces with them, so that while I was teaching they could think about how they would add to their stories).

FIGURE 4.6 Shana's Minilesson Plan for Adding Feelings to Endings

Minilesson Plan (Adding Feelings)

1. Connection

We have been writing lots of wonderful narrative pieces during the last two weeks, but I've noticed something. Some of our pieces just end. Many of our pieces don't tie up our stories; they don't tell our reader what happened or what we were thinking or feeling. We are going to learn how to add feelings to our endings today.

2. Explicit Teaching (Show and Tell)

1. Share my piece about the roller-coaster ride; omit the ending so the children can see it just stops.
2. Tell the story about how Mrs. Graves read the piece and how she didn't like the ending—she felt cheated by the fact that I didn't tell how the story wrapped up. Tell the kids I am going to focus on adding feelings to help me wrap up the writing.
3. Write a revision on the piece with a red pen. Be explicit and discuss my thinking out loud about the revision. "When the roller coaster rolled into the station for an abrupt stop, I felt sick. Then I felt very, very happy. I made it! I rode the roller coaster I was afraid of. I climbed out of the shiny, red car and ran down the ramp to tell my friend. 'I did it, I did it!' I yelled. I was so happy and satisfied."
4. Ask the kids what they think about the piece. Tell them how I feel about the new ending.
5. Create a feelings word chart with the class. Create together.

3. Engagement

Brainstorm with the class what they were feeling at the end of their memory moment. Have them share their ideas at the end of the piece with a writing partner.
Remind them of the feelings chart and to wrap up with an ending that is satisfying.

> Feelings
> Sad, happy, angry,
> Mad, lost, upset

4. Closure

Pick a couple of children to share their writing idea and how the piece would end. Remind them to use the feelings chart. Remind them of the satisfying ending chart.

> Satisfying Endings
> Show what the character feels and thinks.
> ☺☺☹
> Give an example.

How do I know whether I've taught my lesson well and whether the children have understood? I watch what the children are doing when they are writing. Are they pausing to think carefully about the details of their pieces? Are they rereading their middles to themselves, out loud, or to a partner? Have some children written a middle that warrants being shared and talked about with the whole class? If no evidence of comprehension is being demonstrated, I will then reteach and intervene. (Intervention is discussed in Chapter 7.)

Delivery: Presenting the Minilesson

The purpose of a minilesson is to enlarge children's potential and their capacity to learn (Akhavan 2008). When teaching and focusing, always think, "What do I need to show and tell the children to ensure they can do this for themselves?" Focus on helping children connect new learning to previously learned information, develop schemata for absorbing new concepts, and begin to own writing strategies. You want them to not only be aware of strategies but also use them on their own. Instruction unfolds in four steps.

1. Connecting With the Students—Waking Them Up

Great minilessons begin by connecting children to what they are *going* to learn, to *past* learning (prior knowledge), and to *one another*. Whole-group instruction should occur within a community of learners who help one another learn, not a group of individuals who happen to be sitting together! Having the children gather in the class meeting area has several benefits. First, knowing they are coming together for a lesson, they assume a learning mind-set. Second, being able to get up and walk to another part of the room lets the wigglers wiggle and gets everyone's blood flowing. Third, the children reorient themselves to you and one another as they arrange themselves in this new configuration. Your job is to tell them what they are going to learn (state the lesson objective) and how this relates to what they already know or have been learning (connect the objective to prior knowledge).

In other words, you are readying children's brains for learning by having them reconnect with their classmates and with you in an area of the classroom designated as a place where they can interact and express themselves, where they feel safe enough to make mistakes (Englert, Mariage, and Dunsmore 2006; Jensen 2000).

Shana Simpson successfully taught a minilesson about endings to her first graders. In her lesson plan (see Figure 4.6) she connects her students to prior learning: "We have been writing lots of wonderful narrative pieces during the last two weeks, but I've noticed something. Some of our pieces just end. Many of our pieces don't tie up our stories; they don't tell our reader what happened or what we were thinking or feeling. We are going to learn how to add feelings to our endings today." The children knew they were going to add feelings to their endings and that Shana was going to show them how.

2. Explicitly Showing and Telling

Great minilessons are sophisticated show-and-tell sessions. You are showing and telling children something new, something important, something they need to learn. Focus on your measurable objective, and embed the engagement strategies that work best for you. Creating a teaching chart is an essential ingredient here.

After Shana connected her students to what they were going to learn, she dove in, showing them and telling them *how* they were going to add endings to their narrative pieces, unfolding the new learning in deliberate, step-by-step fashion (see Figure 4.6):

■ She displayed a piece of her writing that just stopped, without an engaging ending.
■ She told the students that because another teacher said that the piece just stopped, leaving readers feeling cheated and wondering what happened, she was going to add an ending that focused on her feelings.

FIGURE 4.7 Teaching Chart for Adding Feelings

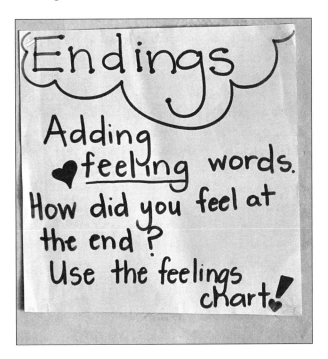

- Using a red pen, she revised the ending to her piece: "When the roller coaster rolled into the station for an abrupt stop, I felt sick. Then I felt very, very happy. I made it! I rode the roller coaster I was afraid of. I climbed out of the shiny, red car and ran down the ramp to tell my friend. 'I did it, I did it!' I yelled. I was so happy and satisfied."
- She asked the students what they thought about the new ending and pointed out how much better she felt the piece was now because she'd added the ending describing her feelings.

Then, to engage the students, she brainstormed feeling words with the class, and they created a chart together.

Finally, to close the lesson, she told the children, "Think about what you are going to write today. How did you feel at the end of the small moment you are describing? Share your thoughts with your writing partner." After the children did this, she pointed to a small chart reminding students to add their feelings to the end of their pieces (see Figure 4.7) and sent them off to write.

3. Thinking and Talking With Engagement

Shana prompted her students to think and talk throughout the minilesson. She talked with them while reading her own writing and asked what they thought of the new ending she added. She encouraged her students to talk together when they were thinking about their own small moments and what feelings they could include in the endings. She also asked the children to brainstorm feeling words and help her create the "Feelings" chart.

Here are some structured ways to engage children during the minilesson:

- *Pair share*: Children are paired with another student (sometimes with a writing partner) and share their thinking together.
- *Think, pair, share*: Before sitting with a partner and sharing thinking together, the children spend a few moments thinking silently about what they will share with their partner. The thinking opportunity gives children time to process new information and decide what to say. It also gives English learners time to think about how to say what they are thinking in English.
- *Write, pair, share*: Children take the time to write down their thinking, or make a revision in their writing, then they partner with another child and share their thinking. The opportunity to write gives children extra thinking time and helps them to jot a note in their writing after listening to the teacher (while the idea is *right there* in their mind).
- *Share and signal*: Children are paired with another student, share their thinking together, and then signal the teacher with a hand gesture (for example, a thumbs-up) when they are done talking and ready to move on. The teacher can prompt students to share about something specific and signal if they have agreement, if they have a new idea, or if they have something to share with the larger group.
- *Think and signal*: Children think alone and then signal the teacher with a hand gesture (for example, a thumbs-up) when they are done thinking and ready to move on.
- *Trio wraparound* or *trio, think, and share*: This is the same as the think, pair, share structured engagement but with three children. Ensure that children sit in a circle, knee-to-knee and eye-to-eye, so that all three children participate equally.
- *Fishbowl discussion*: The teacher invites a few children to share their thinking with the entire class. These children are organized in a small group in front of the class and then they participate in a discussion with the teacher facilitating. The teacher helps the children think aloud and ensures that the students are learning from one another's thinking and decision making about their writing.

4. Closing or Transitioning

At the end of the lesson, you need to remind children what you have just taught them, tell them what you have showed them. Then send them off to write. Shana concluded her lesson by asking her students to try adding feelings to the end of their pieces to create a satisfying ending. She directed their attention to the charts she created, pointing to specific words or phrases and running her hand beneath sentences stating what they needed to think about.

Assessment: Checking for Understanding

You need to know if your students have understood your teaching. Watch their body language. Are they looking at you? Do they appear attentive? Do all the children contribute ideas or only a few? Listen to the conversations children have with one another. Do any of them need to be redirected? You can even ask explicitly whether they understand something, having them signal with a thumbs-up if they do, a thumbs-down if they don't.

Most important, does the children's writing reflect the concept, strategy, or skill they were taught? For example, Parker added, *I was really, really mad at Jacky that he got dirty again [because] it was my turn to wash Jacky* to his piece (see Figure 4.8), indicating that he understood what he had been asked to do.

Here are some structured ways to check children's understanding:

- *Think and signal*: See previous explanation on page 56. Focus on children's understanding of an idea or information, rather than only on children's thinking and discussion.
- *Write and show (using whiteboards)*: Each child writes his answer or thought on a whiteboard and holds it up for the teacher to see. Students might write in response to a question posed by the teacher or by the class, or respond to an invitation to try out a writing skill like using dialogue or using beautiful language in a sentence. The children are applying a skill or idea taught in the minilesson. The focus is on the teacher checking for the children's understanding of something she taught in the minilesson.
- *Yes/no cards*: The teacher prepares index cards with *yes* written on one side and *no* written on the opposite side. Each child holds up a card with the correct side showing in response to a teacher prompt. The focus is on the teacher checking for the children's understanding of something he taught in the minilesson. The teacher can then follow up with the children to ensure learning.
- *Happy/sad face cards*: The teacher prepares index cards with a happy face on one side and a sad face on the opposite side. The cards are used in the same manner as the yes/no cards, where the happy face represents understanding and the sad face represents confusion or lack of understanding.
- *Fist to five*: Children indicate their level of understanding of a new idea or thinking when prompted by the teacher. The number of fingers a child holds up represents her level of understanding. A fist represents a 0 level, or confusion, and a 5 represents full understanding.
- *Graffiti board*: Post a piece of chart paper with a statement or question on it related to the writing minilesson. The children write, scribble, or note their thinking with pens, markers, or crayons on the blank space below the heading you wrote. The children can graffiti the chart with their thinking about the prompt to indicate their level of understanding. Another way a graffiti board can be used is for children to record facts about what they know. They can list what they know or have learned about the topic the you listed in the heading.

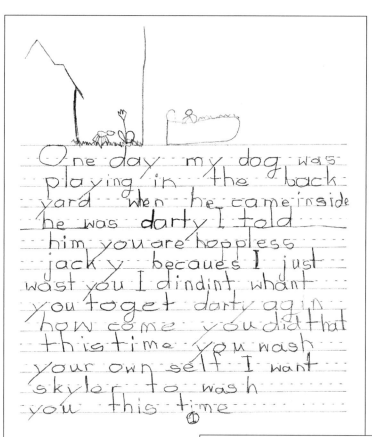

FIGURE 4.8 Parker's Piece About His Dog Jacky

One day my dog was playing in the back yard when he came inside he was darty I told him you are hoopless jacky becaues I just wast you I dindint whant you toget darty agin how come you did that this time you wash your own self I want skyler to wash you this time ①

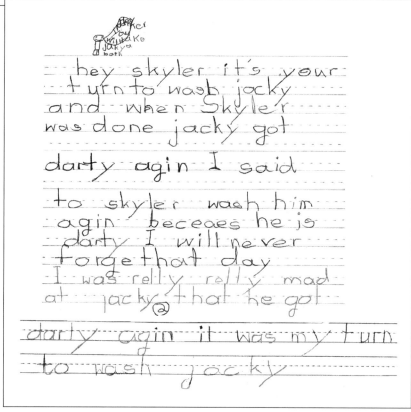

hey skyler it's your turn to wash jacky and when Skyler was done jacky got darty agin I said to skyler wash him agin beceaes he is darty I will never forge that day I was relly relly mad at jacky ② that he got darty agin it was my turn to wash jacky

Guided Instruction

Guided instruction is just another name for an explicit, purposeful mini-lesson (Fisher and Frey 2008; Graham and Harris 2007). Guided instruction

- engages students by starting at the point they've reached in developing their knowledge and helping them own their learning
- prompts students to think on their own instead of waiting for someone else to tell them what to think or how to think
- helps students develop knowledge in stages, gradually becoming responsible for their own learning
- focuses on student learning and students' needs

Guided instruction moves along a continuum from the early stages of teaching, in which you show, tell, demonstrate, guide, and model, and children attempt, try, think, and focus, to later stages of teaching, in which you remind, add, revisit, and enhance, and children understand, own, and write with fluency and joy.

Figure 4.9 is a graphic depiction of the release of responsibility that occurs during explicit, purposeful writing instruction. (It's a companion to the release-of-responsibility model presented in *Teaching Reading in a Title I School, K–3* [Akhavan 2008] on page 73.) As children develop their writing abilities, your instruction changes in response to their changing needs.

FIGURE 4.9   Release-of-Responsibility Model

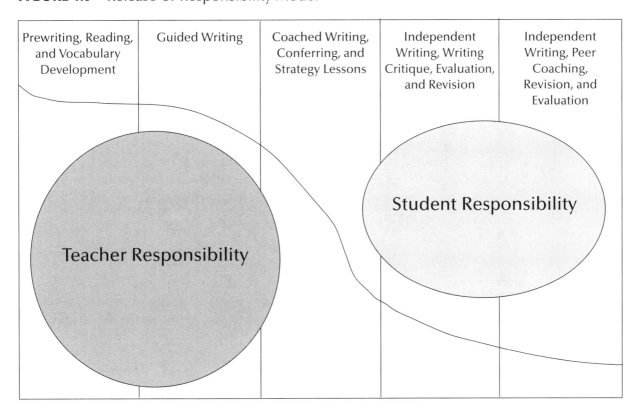

| Prewriting, Reading, and Vocabulary Development | Guided Writing | Coached Writing, Conferring, and Strategy Lessons | Independent Writing, Writing Critique, Evaluation, and Revision | Independent Writing, Peer Coaching, Revision, and Evaluation |

Teacher Responsibility

Student Responsibility

When you present scaffolded reading and writing instruction, your students will exhibit predictable classroom behavior and you will be able to help them grow and develop their thinking-and-doing muscles related to reading, writing about reading, and writing specific genres.

Through scaffolding, your students' abilities will grow. At first they may not know how to write effective narratives, *but you will show them how.* They may not know how to revise their writing to include a specific feature or use correct conventions, *but you will show them how.* Remember: first tell, then show, then tell what you showed to make sure they understand. After the lesson, move around the room, watching the children work independently and in groups. Pair them with a buddy so they can help each other. Eventually they will control the genres and strategies you've taught them, solidify their knowledge of conventions, and express themselves fluently in writing. First hang on, then let go.

Why Teaching Matters—Desperately

Our instruction matters more than we give ourselves credit for (or may sometimes hope it does). Without instruction there is no learning. Until students learn, we have not accomplished what we have set out to do, which is to make a difference in children's lives. When students have a series of ineffective teachers, they know less than other students *because they were taught less.* Some children are never able to close that gap (Haycock 2001).

I fretted for years about being an effective teacher. I worried while driving home from school, as I took my bedtime shower, when I couldn't sleep: *Did I do good work today?* I evaluated my teaching and my students' learning relentlessly. I know now that there are no absolutes but that as long as I focus and make sure I am teaching explicitly what I want students to *know* and *know how to do*, I am teaching well and effectively.

Allow yourself to grow. Get into the minilesson canoe and paddle along until you feel more comfortable being direct, brief, and concise. If you are already presenting minilessons, think of ways you can increase your students' engagement or create more effective teaching charts. Give yourself time and room to make mistakes, explore new ways of teaching, and most important, kidwatch. Your students will learn more and be able to do more. I guarantee it.

CHAPTER FIVE

Write from Day One
Focused and Guided Writing Practice

Children should write every day. Better writers are better readers, read more, and produce more well developed and mature writing. "When we spend time teaching children to write, we are improving their reading skills, and vice versa."

NATIONAL WRITING PROJECT AND NAGIN,
Because Writing Matters

Children don't learn to write without time to write. Sounds self-evident, doesn't it? Surprisingly enough, this is a precept we ignore every day in our classrooms. Because we are perhaps squeezed for time, because we are slightly uncomfortable teaching writing, because we feel pressured to have our students fill out the thick booklet of worksheets that comes with our writing program, our students are not writing.

Teaching alone isn't enough to ensure our children learn to write. Writing matters, and because it does, children need to write every day. If you are wondering how you are going to accomplish that, or if you are ready to stop reading because giving children time "just to write" in your classroom might induce apoplexy in your administrator, keep breathing and then keep reading.

Writing, Not Worksheets

Worksheets are no substitute for the experience of writing. "But," you may be wondering, "how am I going to reinforce my teaching without assigning worksheets or writing exercises?" By having your students write whole pieces of text for a purpose. Ask them to write narratives and reports and poetry that make their hearts sing and pull their minds to attention.

When writing whole pieces, children

■ have a genuine reason to write
■ are writing to an audience

- can revise and review their purpose for writing
- focus on genre
- share ideas with peers
- focus on feedback

Writing authentic texts is more motivating and engaging than participating in writing activities and grammar drills or filling in the blanks on a worksheet. Children learn to write successfully when there is a proper balance between process and product, when they create a text they can read and share with others.

Begin with a memory moment. It doesn't have to be about a big trip or an earth-shaking discovery. Darchea wrote about going to Save Mart (a grocery store) with her father (see Figure 5.1).

FIGURE 5.1 Darchea's Piece on Grocery Shopping

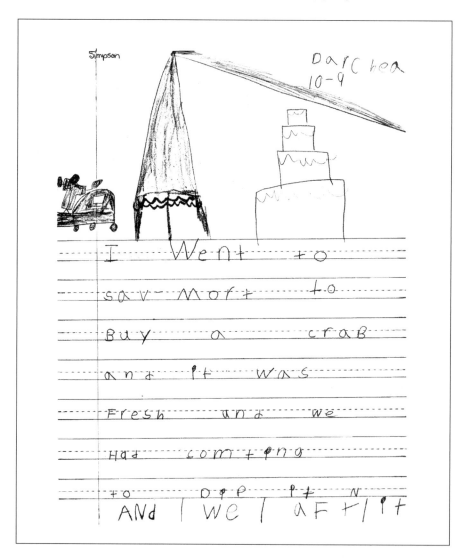

Practice That Works

Writing works when it is connected to your minilessons. When you give your students ample time to practice, with your guidance, you help them regulate their own writing strategies, let them immediately attempt the genres they are learning about, and make sure they understand the connection between a skill you've taught, like sounding out a word to write it down, and writing a whole text. While your students are writing, you are coaching them—pulling together a small group of students and reteaching the minilesson objective, helping children rethink their writing, suggesting how they can make their writing more effective—while making sure they are doing the thinking, not relying on you to think for them.

Effective practice flows from the minilesson and is focused or guided. How and what you expect children to do molds and shapes the day's writing. And each and every writing session should be followed by sharing and closure—a wrap-up. To recap, then, your writing workshop has three major sections:

- a minilesson (see Chapter 4)
- a period in which students practice their writing with peers or independently
- a sharing and wrap-up session

An effective workshop requires between forty and sixty minutes: five to fifteen minutes for the minilesson, a writing period of at least fifteen minutes but preferably thirty minutes or more, and a sharing and wrap-up session of five or ten minutes.

The Writing Portion of Writing Workshop

The writing your students do in a workshop flows from the minilesson— what you taught in the minilesson is what children now work on with peers or independently. This moves naturally from focused practice, in which children receive more direct, scaffolded help from you, to guided practice, when you move around the classroom helping specific students focus and refocus on the task at hand.

Some people mistakenly believe that a workshop doesn't include focused practice—that children just write, write, write, and by the end are able to do so effectively. But research tells us learning doesn't work this way. Children need explicit teaching to learn writing strategies (Harris and Graham 1996; National Writing Project and Nagin 2006). They need help learning the cognitive aspects of writing, focusing on the deliberate use of strategies until they become automatic. This kind of practice isn't linear and performed in lockstep but rather cyclical, just as learning is. Children try out their writing muscles, exercise them, in order to be able to write with stamina as they think about and understand the choices available to them. Children need help with skills they haven't yet completely mastered. You want to engage young children, entice them to want to write, get them to feel the anticipation and commitment necessary to not be afraid to write words on the page.

Practicing writing in conjunction with you and their peers helps children construct knowledge for themselves. They need the opportunity to talk about how to write, about the writing you model for them, about their writing process, and about one another's writing. Thinking about these texts and ideas helps them develop their understanding of writing processes and practices (New Standards Speaking and Listening Committee 2001; Englert, Mariage, and Dunsmore 2006). Sometimes you'll create opportunities for focused, structured practice; other times you'll help them as they work on a piece independently.

During focused practice you may get the attention of the whole class or a small group and redirect their thinking; highlight how a particular child has attempted a strategy or skill; or celebrate additional examples of craft, voice, and organization. In essence, you are reteaching the minilesson to make sure children really know and understand an idea or strategy before they have time to learn it incorrectly. Effective, focused practice scaffolds all children's writing skills and ensures that even struggling writers are successful. You want all your students eventually to write on their own, as you coach, nurture, and celebrate their successes.

During guided practice you confer with students one-on-one, in pairs, or in small groups. You check on their writing and their thinking about their writing. You coach them while they are working—watch them write, notice what they can do and what they still need help doing, reinforce their attempts to use writing strategies, explain what they are doing and why it works (McKeough et al. 2007; Bereiter and Scardamalia 2006). If children are stuck, you encourage them to think about what they know about writing and gently show them what to do. At the end of a conference, you may give each child a goal to focus on.

Organizing the Workshop for Focused and Guided Practice

You'll organize the writing portion of the workshop slightly differently, depending on whether you're providing focused or guided practice. The left side of Figure 5.2 lists actions you can take when your students need the strategic scaffolds provided by focused practice. The right side describes guided practice—actions you can take when students are able to work independently. Depending on your students' needs, you may provide scaffolds in both kinds of practice.

If a large number of children require focused practice, you might teach a short minilesson outlining what you are going to work on together as a class, then choose from a variety of scaffolds that support young writers: sentence strips, charts, interactive writing, paired writing, and small-group strategy or skill lessons and collaborative writing.

FIGURE 5.2 Components of Focused and Guided Practice

Focused Practice	Guided Practice
Sentence-strip writing	Independent writing
Chart writing	Stretching to spell
Interactive writing	Writing planning and idea development
Partner writing	
Modeled strategy or skill writing	Choosing writing goals
Drawing and labeling	Conferring on writing skills or strategies
Planning writing	Conferring about writing organization
Word card–supported writing	
Small-group modeled writing	Conferring about genre knowledge and development
	First draft focus
	Dictionary and thesaurus use

If you differentiate instruction, choose scaffolds from the left side of the graphic to support your struggling writers, and use the coaching actions on the right side to help more proficient children own writing strategies and content knowledge.

The teacher and student actions on the guided practice side of Figure 5.2 help you release responsibility for learning to your students. You model, teach, show, and tell during the minilesson and then, in one-on-one and small-group conferences, coach children to think through how to use these strategies and concepts and try them out. Guided practice focuses on children's independent use of writing strategies. You sit down and confer with children, checking on how their writing is going and guiding their learning. Avoid the temptation to fix the writing yourself; instead, coach these young writers to recognize and fix the problems on their own.

When we fix the writing, we sit with the child, perhaps with a red pen in hand, and add or subtract words to suit our needs. When we coach a young writer to recognize and fix problems on her own, we sit with the child and help her think through the piece. Does the writing have the elements you have taught and are aiming for each child to know and be able to control on her own? If not, then discuss what is present in the writing and what might be missing, then brainstorm with the child how she could fix it, and let the child take the pen or pencil and make the changes on her own.

Sharing and Wrapping Up

The sharing session at the end of the workshop is your opportunity to drive home your main teaching point before moving on, to bring things to a close and help your students reflect on what they've learned. Begin by reminding children about the day's lesson—what you discussed and what they have been working on. Redirect their attention to the chart you created.

Then ask for volunteers (or ask specific students) to share their writing. As they do, offer positive comments that highlight the lesson's objective and reinforce the learning that has taken place:

- "Notice how Maria stretched her sounds while writing her story."
- "Notice how José used an engaging beginning to capture the reader's attention."
- "Jessica focused on organizing structure today; her narrative has a beginning, a middle, and an end."

An individual child's writing can be a springboard for a whole-class discussion, but make sure that your comments validate all the children. After you comment, ask the children to talk about what they thought or experienced while they were writing, so they can teach and learn from one another. (Reinforcing the teaching point and validating the children's work takes three or four minutes; spend the remainder of the time having children share their thinking.)

You can also wrap up the workshop by having students share their writing and thinking in small groups of three or four or with a buddy. Ask them to share one specific thing they tried in their writing that day. Giving them time to articulate their thinking out loud leads to purposeful talk and lets children practice and develop language skills.

During the wrap-up, you

- reinforce the day's teaching point
- validate the writing and thinking of all children
- remind students how to *own* a strategy
- tell a bit about what will happen during the next workshop

Scaffolds That Support Young Writers

"OK, let's get started," Lori whispers at the end of her minilesson. Immediately the children spread themselves around the classroom. Some gather in the area near the bookshelves, take a clipboard, press down on the metal clip at the top, and slide their writing paper underneath. Others nestle at their desk, writing folder open, word list tucked in the front pocket, ready to explore. Still others gather at the reading table, pulling markers and erasers from the materials basket. The children are focused; their energy is tangible.

What the children are writing is as different as where they've settled. Mercedes, an English learner who has been in the United States a little over six months, is writing on paper that includes a large box for an illustration. She draws a picture showing herself, her sister, a cake, and a dog near the cake. She and her sister have big smiles on their faces. Under this picture (using phonetic spelling and copying some words from cards in her writing folder), she writes, *I like wn mi str cake fl* [*I like when my sister's cake fell*].

Angela is writing on green paper that has large lines drawn across most of the page and a small box for a picture at the top. (Lori's students use color-coded writing paper—green for the beginning of the piece, yellow for the middle of the piece, and pink for the end of the piece.) The chart in Figure 5.3, which is linked with the colored paper, prompts Angela to introduce characters and grab the reader with details.

Sean has settled at his desk, with *Toot and Puddle: The New Friend*, by Holly Hobbie (2004)—a book from the "Favorites" basket—lying on his desk next to his writing paper. A few days earlier, Lori pointed out how the author of this book used little details to make the friendship between the characters come alive and seem real. Sean opens the text and looks intensely at the page Lori highlighted in her minilesson. He scans the picture, closes the book, and begins drawing on paper that includes a large area for illustrations. Later he labels one of the people in the picture with the words

FIGURE 5.3 Color-Coded Teaching Chart on Narrative Organization

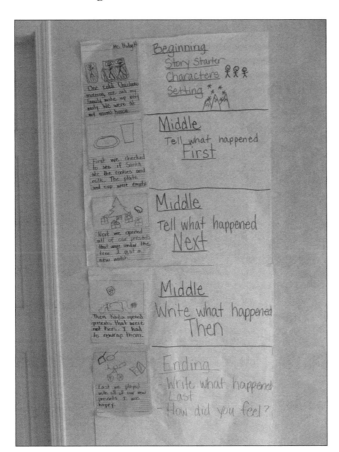

mi bs friend, sounding out the words *my* and *best* and copying *friend* from the word wall. (Mentor texts help young children develop skills related to the craft of writing, as well as a sense of story.)

Lori is using a variety of scaffolds to support her young writers. You can, too:

■ *Writing folders*: Choose folders with two pockets. Label one side "My Writing" and the other "My Writing Resources." Children place current writing pieces in the "My Writing" pocket and writing scaffolds like sound-spelling cards, word cards, or personal dictionaries in the "My Writing Resources" pocket. (Blackline master for My Favorite Word Bank is included in the appendix.)

■ *Writing paper*: Set up a writing station where children can choose paper that you have modeled how to use in minilessons. Kinds of appropriate writing paper, depending on children's grade level and writing readiness, include sheets of blank white paper, sheets of lined white paper, paper with spaces for illustrations, sheets of lined paper in three colors to help children organize their writing, and binder paper.

Word cards: Word cards and word rings help children spell words they use frequently (for example, see the List of 100 Most Frequently Used Words in the appendix). Write these words on index cards held together on a

FIGURE 5.4 Student Dictionary

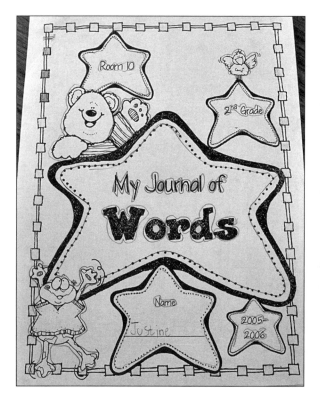
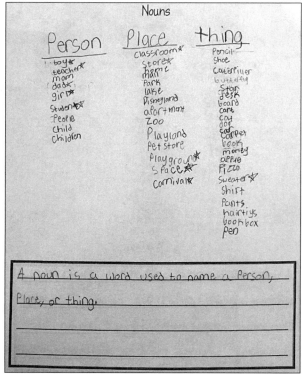

large metal ring (or store them in a plastic bag). A blackline master may be created using index cards. Use a hole punch to make a hole in the upper-left corner and connect cards together with a metal ring or strong string.

- *Planning paper* (see appendix)
- *Add-on writing paper* (see appendix)
- *"My Favorite Word Bank" list* (see appendix)
- *Student dictionaries* (see the examples in Figure 5.4)
- *Bubblegum stretch cards* (see appendix)

FIGURE 5.5   Deven's Narrative

With the help of scaffolds like these, your students will be able to write successfully, with focus and skill; they will understand how to express themselves, make their words fly. Look how well Deven expresses himself in his narrative "My Dog" (Figure 5.5) and how effectively Isaiah arranges the words of his poem "Swing" (Figure 5.6).

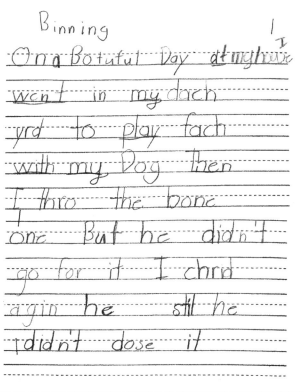

FIGURE 5.5 Deven's Narrative (*continued*)

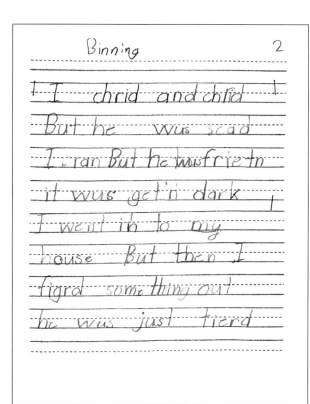

[Page 2]

Binning   2

I chrid and chrid
But he wus scad
I ran But he wus frie tn
it wus get'n dark
I went in to my
house But then I
figrd some thing out
he wus just tierd

[Page 3]

                        3
        Binning
it was morning
this time I thro
it foru But hestildin
doit But then I calledout
to see if he wud
cum to me But he
didn't come I wus
geting aegre But I didn't
stop

[Page 4]

Middle   4
I chrid every thing
what Dog Do But
he didn't do inc Thing
But I thot of my
Dog chacing a Cat
it would be fun
I Put my cat next
to my Dog he didn't doeneu
thing

FIGURE 5.5 Deven's Narrative (*continued*)

Middle   5

I mant my
Dog chaesing my cat
I cont Blev it
my Dog shold be
chaesing my cat I
yelled chaes my cat
I said But he sick
I said niele

End   6

Ples will you come
to me and he
came to me I
thro the bone
hiey up in to the
arey he jumped
and cot it it was
funny sow much
I like my Dog

FIGURE 5.6 Isaiah's Poem

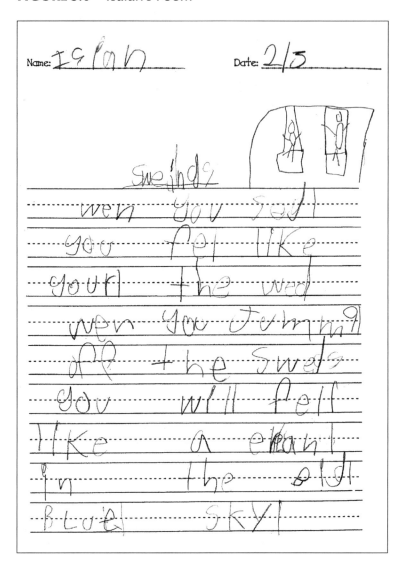

Name: Isiah   Date: 2/5

Sweinde
wen you sed
you fel like
yourl the wed
wen you Jumping
off the swets
you will fell
like a elfant
in the old
Blue sky

CHAPTER SIX

<hr>

Launching and Leading Students' Writing Development
Teaching Strategies and Skills

Teach writing? Oh, not me, I'm not a good writer.

How that statement resonates with me. However, when I sit down to help a teacher teach writing, I think, *Well, why* not *me?* We don't have to be writing experts to teach writing. We don't have to be *perfect* at teaching writing; we just have to make it part of our curriculum and then encourage and nurture writing throughout the year. Our students don't have to be perfect at writing, either; they only need to get better at it, and all children can grow. Launching writing instruction is sometimes the hardest part, but once we've done so we are often unsure whether we are doing it well or getting good results.

Any thought of perfection is what we have to avoid: if we concentrate too hard on the shoulds, musts, and have-tos, we can easily leave our students confused and frustrated. Some children will learn to write but might not learn to write with voice until they are older. Some children won't control the skill of descriptive writing, but that doesn't mean they haven't made progress or that their writing doesn't meet an assessment standard. When we look for specific words used or points made in a child's piece, we may miss the wonderful things a child does know how to do. So leave *perfect* behind as you plan how to launch writing with your students and help them develop the necessary strategies and skills.

Helping Children Understand Genres

Think of yourself as the tour guide and the genre as the city or country you're leading people through. Help children understand what a genre entails: purpose, text structure, word use. Show children what narrative looks like and sounds like; how poetry looks, sounds, and feels when spoken; how expository text has its own guidelines, conventions, and clues to meaning. *Guide your students not to discovery but to understanding.*

Does that last statement surprise you, perhaps ruffle your feathers? Honestly, we don't have enough time to prompt children to discover the joy of knowledge; we have to teach them. If we are working with children who may not (yet) have all the academic learning, experiences, or understanding they need, we have to create lessons and classroom experiences that teach them. We need to teach the children *how* to write, problem solve, build the stamina to draft, revise, and edit. Let the discovery come on its own, from the inside: the joy children feel when they get it, when they prepare a report they're proud of, when they narrate a favorite memory that resonates beyond the memory itself.

To be able to teach genre structure, you need to know the general definitions and descriptions and then adjust them to the age and grade level of the children in your class. A map is helpful to anyone navigating territory, whether new or familiar. It never hurts to revisit genre structure—I am usually reminded of information I have forgotten, which helps me make my instruction more powerful, or I learn something new, a little gift.

Mapping Genres for Instruction

Remember that you are leaving behind the musts, shoulds, and have-tos, so a map is not gospel—it's a guide. When you expect children to create cookie-cutter responses to literature or narratives that look very similar to the narratives about pumpkin picking your students produced *last year* during November, you are on the wrong track. A genre map helps you plan instruction that is effective, purposeful, and gets results (Akhavan 2004).

Whatever the genre, the writing the children produce needs to be created for a purpose: to be read and shared by an audience. Applying a genre map to an artificial activity—asking children to write a narrative about vacation when they live in a tough neighborhood and are often relieved that vacation is over and they can go back to the "something other" of school, for example—makes writing feel inauthentic. To prompt purposeful writing, there is one must you *do* need to follow: you *must* avoid applying genre maps to hollow writing prompts or activities. Instead, delve into the rich experience of teaching children to write authentic pieces within the context of the writing process—developing topics, drafting, revising, editing, and publishing.

Although there are a large number of genres to choose from, this chapter focuses on the six most often connected to state standards and writing programs for young children:

■ narrative, or memory moment, writing

■ report, or informational, writing

■ procedural, or how-to, writing

■ writing in response to literature

■ letter writing

■ poetry

Chapter Six

Presenting a genre unit of study lets you teach the writing process naturally. As the unit unfolds, you guide children through the writing process: nurturing an idea, drafting, revising, editing, and publishing. Children need to know how to choose a topic or idea and nurture that idea, and they need to understand that writing is revision, that it needs to be edited for publication. Taking nine or ten pieces through the writing process over the course of an academic year gives children a wealth of practice composing, revising and revisioning their work, and preparing it for an audience.

The writing process isn't linear. Children will begin many, many drafts. They will write to explore ideas and put their thoughts on paper. They will choose one of their many drafts to edit and publish. When they edit and prepare a piece for presentation, remember to teach the writer, not the writing. Don't have children fix every mistake; have them edit in connection with what you have taught them, what you have focused on. Require that they correctly use punctuation you've taught them; allow them to spell stretched words phonetically. The point isn't perfection; the point is to teach them about preparing writing for an audience.

If you want children to become so enamored with learning to write that they can't help plunging in when you send them off after the minilesson, you have to show them the endless satisfaction and rewards of writing well. Do this with the way you launch the unit and then with the way you lead children through it. Model with joy and assurance, without doubting yourself. Believe so strongly in your students that they won't be able to help themselves, they will love to write.

When launching and leading any genre unit, focus on what children *learn* from your instruction, then add to their learning by teaching new information and connecting this new learning to their previous learning.

Narratives

Figure 6.1 is a map of the narrative writing genre.

Launching the Learning

- Have students read narratives written by published authors and student authors.
- Gather many narrative books and place them around the classroom.
- Place your favorite narratives in a big basket near your teaching chair and easel and use them as examples.
- Read several narrative books aloud. Talk about what you notice in a book as a writer (the structure, the wondrous language, the writing craft, the author's voice).
- Read memoirs to the children to show the difference between story and personal narrative.
- Explain the difference between story and personal narrative.

FIGURE 6.1 Narrative Genre Map

	Description
Purpose of Narrative	Tells a story. A personal narrative is autobiographical writing that shares specific meaning with the reader.
Characteristics	Employs story structure. Has clear beginning, middle, and end. Characters are well developed (in personal narrative, characters include the self). Shares a memory experience, including thoughts and feelings. Analyzes the significance or impact of an event, decision, or experience. Focuses on a specific experience or an extended period of time in a person's life. Personal narrative has a narrow focus; it is written about a small scope of time. Engages the reader. Includes sensory detail and specific language to develop plot and character. Establishes a situation, plot, point of view, setting, and conflict.
Uses/Types	Story Personal narrative Memoir Autobiography
Organization	Beginning, middle, and end. Uses event words to show passage of time. Has engaging beginning to hook the reader. Satisfying ending brings closure to the piece. Dialogue can be between people or be writer's inner thoughts. Includes writer's thoughts and feelings. Presents information chronologically. Ending can include a reflection.
Conventions or Techniques	Tell story from your own life. Follow a time line with your story. Can use flashback memories to provide detail. Stories from own life are often told in first person (*I*). Stories told through observation, or another's perspective, are told in third person (*he/she*). Use dialogue to show actions, thoughts, and feelings of characters. Include writer's thoughts and feelings. Develop context through descriptive techniques. Exclude extraneous detail. Develop pacing through sentence variety. Show, don't tell, to develop detail. Use sensory details to create emotion and mood. Magnify the moment to slow down narrative action and create visual picture in reader's mind.

FIGURE 6.2 Teaching Charts for Narrative
Writing Unit

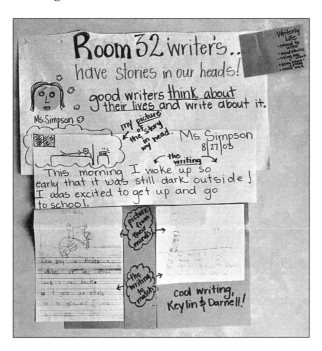

- Teach children that the best writing is about everyday moments.
- Keep it small. Teach children to think of a moment to write about.
- Model writing your memory moment, a personal narrative that focuses on a moment in time.

Figure 6.2 presents an example of a teaching chart created at the beginning of a narrative unit of study.

Leading the Learning

- Teach children how narratives are organized: beginning, middle, end.
- Model writing engaging beginnings and satisfying endings.
- Show children how to write with details and emotions.
- Model focusing on small details to engage readers.
- Find and celebrate literary language and wondrous words in published books.
- Create a literary language book or a literary language wall.
- Teach dialogue and prompt your students to think of what people did and said during their memory moments.
- Show children how to revise, how to add details to their writing.

Figure 6.3 presents examples of teaching charts used to extend learning during a narrative unit of study.

FIGURE 6.3   More Teaching Charts for Narrative Writing Unit

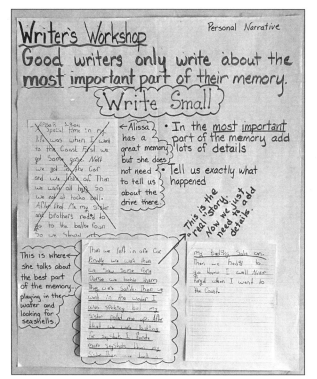

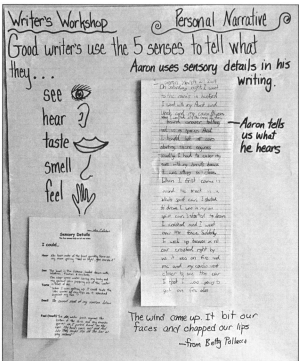

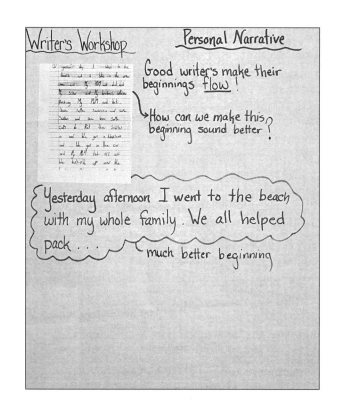

Writing Outcomes

What should student writing look like and sound like at your grade level? While it is most important to focus on what your children are learning and help them further their abilities, looking at representative pieces of children's writing gives you something to teach toward.

The following writing samples are examples of end-of-the-year personal narratives that focus on writing small—that is, sharing a memory moment. These children wrote each and every day, and their ability to express themselves shines through. The children attended a Title I school and had few academic advantages.

Robert's Narrative (Kindergarten) (Figure 6.4)

One day my mom and my dad got married. It was daytime. It was hot. The sun was out. I was standing on the middle step then Hanna was singing, then Michael gave the ring to me. I gave the ring to the lord. Then Kim kissed my dad on the lips. Then it was over. I played and I ran. I did not know there was a cactus. I ran through the cactus. I was bleeding. I went into the bathroom. I wiped my leg. It stopped bleeding. I was better. I was walking when I was playing. Then all the people left.

Sean's Narrative (First Grade)

The Barbecue

One weekend in March we had a barbecue with my mom, dad, sister, and brother. My sister's name is Jenny and she is 14. My brother's name is Cesar and he is 12. "Jenny, Cesar, Sean, come and eat," my mom said. We ate hamburgers and we ate hot dogs. Mmmmm. Crunch. After we ate I jumped into the pool. Whoopee! I played a game. You have to go under the people's legs. If you touch their legs you are it. Then I jumped into the pool 13 times. My brother jumped lots of times. He jumped in 13 times. I jumped on the diving board. It was fun. I touched the ground with my feet. I got a little circle. I threw it into the pool. Plop. I will never forget when I had a barbecue with my family. I was feeling happy because I have a nice mom and dad and brother and sister. (See the beginning of Sean's narrative in Figure 6.5.)

Marky's Narrative (Second Grade)

He's Gone

Last October me and my mom went to Delano for a fair. On the way my mom told me about my brother. She said, "When I had your brother, it was right here in Delano."

I asked, "What happened to him?"

FIGURE 6.4 Robert's Narrative

Name: Robert   Date: 5-17-

WuN boy MY MoM
ANb MY Dad got
MeryD It was
daY tEM I WastoT
The SuN was
Awt. I was staNii
oN The MiDol stel
ThiN HaNNa was
SeiNg geNg

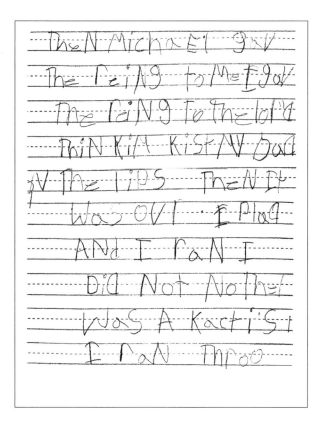

TheN MichaEl gav
The reiNg to Me I gov
The reiNg to the loT'd
ThiNKiN KisT NY DaD
gV The liDS TheN It
was ovT I PloYd
ANd I raN I
DiD Not No theT
was A KactiS t
I raN Throo

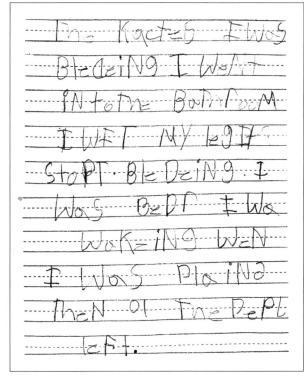

The KacteS ElwaS
BleDeiNg I weNt
iNtothe BaThrooM
I wET MY leDT
StoPT BleDeiNg I
was BeDT I Wa
WaKeiNg WeN
I lwas PlaiNg
TheN ol The PePL
leFt.

FIGURE 6.5 Sean's Narrative—First Two Pages

One weekend in March we had a barbeque with my mom, dad, sister, and brother.

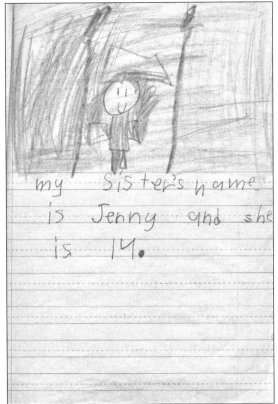

my sister's name is Jenny and she is 14.

She said, "He died before his first birthday." She also said that the day after he was buried at the cemetery her neighbor said, "I always hear a baby cry." My mom told him, "I don't have a baby anymore."

I had a feeling at that part of the story that might be his spirit. I said, "Let's stop at that store." So we stopped at the store, we stopped in, and when we came out we had peach-colored roses. And I asked my mom if we can give the flowers to Robert. So we took off to Delano Cemetery.

When my mom saw his name she started to cry. I think she missed Robert. He was her first son before I was born. Then my mom told him, "This is your brother, Robert; his name is Marky. I hope you're happy." I started to cry. I wondered, How did he die? Was he born too small? Or did he get sick? I thought, If only I was there then I'll know the answer.

Then my mom said, "Come on, Marky, let's go to the fair."

I said, "It's OK, this is better than a fair 'cause this is special." And I will never forget that day I learned about my brother. (See Figure 6.6.)

FIGURE 6.6 Marky's Narrative

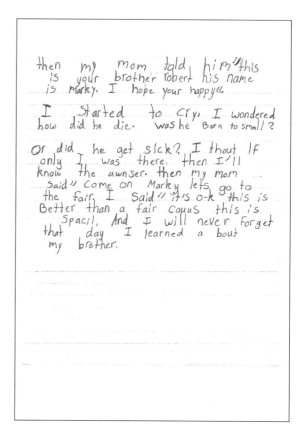

Marc 3-4o

He's Gone

Last October me and my mom went to Dalano for a fair. On the way MY Mom told me about my Brother. She Said" when I had your Brother it was right here in Dalano." I asked" what hapend to him"? She Said" he dide befor his first birthday. She also Said " the day after he was beryd at the Semetery. her naibber Said" I always here a baby cry. My Mom told him " I Dont have a baby anymore. I had A feling at that part of the Story that might be his spiret. I Said " Lets stop at that store.
So we stoped at the store we Stoped in and when we came out we had peach colered roses. And I asked My Mom if we can give the flowers to Robert.

So we tault off to Dalano Semetery. When my mom saw his name she Started to cry. I think She missed Robert. he was her first son befor I was born.

then my mom told him" this is your brother robert his name is marky. I hope your happy".

I Started to cry. I wondered how did he die. was he Born to small?

Or did he get sick?. I thout If only I was there, then I'll know the awnser. then my mom Said" Come on Marky lets go to the fair. I Said " it's o-k this is Better than a fair cauus this is Spacil, And I will never forget that day I learned about my brother.

Roselle's Narrative (Third Grade)

Leaving the Country: A True Story

One beautiful day, when I was just 3 years old, my family lived in a country with flowers that mostly grow a lot and grass that are tall but mostly the country was beautiful. The day came when my mom said, "We are going to leave this country because it was a terrible place and it's ruined forever." I was so sad leaving the country, it made me get stuck of a chair so I didn't have to leave.

And when the stars sparkled in the sky. The next day before daybreak we were packing and I just wanted to drink water but I had to keep going on and on and on. I thought that if my mom lets me rest, then I could go outside and get flowers that were still in our big backyard. So she said yes. I picked the flowers that will end forever and still remember my country and everything else.

By morning we're at the airport and I had my flowers in my suitcase. I asked, "May we sit down? I need to rest," but we had to keep going. I said, "Mom, can I say something to you and it is important?" So I said, "Can we stay here!" but she said no!

So when we were on the airplane I fell asleep and looked in my mind, and saw the good times and everything else. When we finally reached America I opened my suitcase, and right in the middle was the flowers that sparkled like moon, stars, and sun. (See Figure 6.7.)

Chapter Six

FIGURE 6.7 Roselle's Narrative

Leaving
The
Country
A True Story

By Roselle

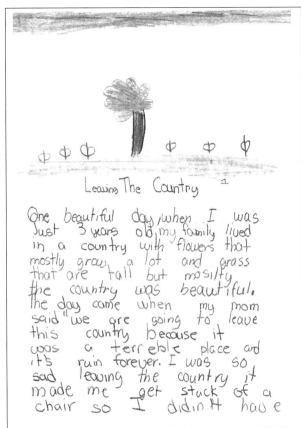

Leaving The Country   1

One beautiful day, when I was
Just 3 years old, my family lived
in a country with flowers that
mostly grow a lot and grass
that are tall but mostly
the country was beautiful.
The day come when my mom
said "we are going to leave
this country because it
was a terreble place and
its ruin forever. I was so
sad leaving the country it
made me get stuck of a
chair so I didintt have

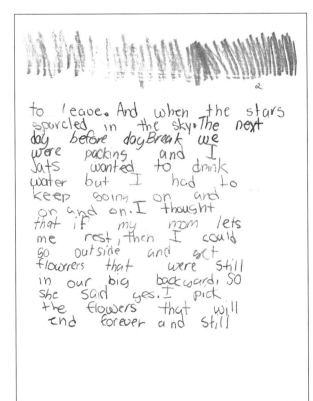

to leave. And when the stars
sparcled in the sky. The next
day before dayBreak we
were packing and I
Jats wanted to drink
water but I had to
keep going on and
on and on. I thought
that if my mom lets
me rest, then I could
go outside and get
flowers that were still
in our big backyard. So
she said yes. I pick
the flowers that will
end forever and still

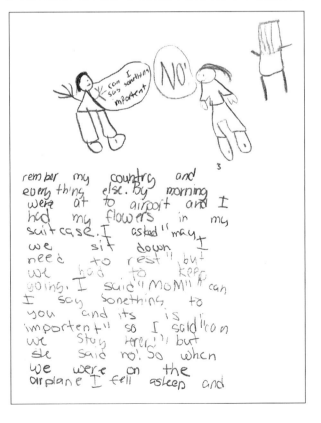

rember my country and
everything else. By morning
were at to airport and I
had my flowers in my
suitcase. I asked "may we
sit down I
need to rest" but
we had to keep
going. I said "MOM!" "can
I say something to
you and its is
importent" so I said "can
we stay here!" but
she said no! So when
we were on the
airplane I fell asleep and

FIGURE 6.7 Roselle's Narrative *(continued)*

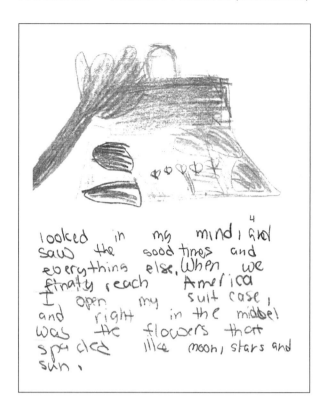

looked in my mind, and
saw the good times and
everything else. When we
finally reach America
I open my suit case,
and right in the middel
was the flowers that
sparcled like moon, stars and
sun.

Informational Reports

Most of the writing your students will do throughout their lives will be to convey information, so introducing informational reports in the early grades and teaching the skills needed to write them successfully is essential (Bender 2007). Begin by introducing children to various nonfiction genres, structures, and conventions and teaching them how to read and learn from nonfiction texts. Then model how to use this knowledge to write a simple report. Focus your instruction on what children in *this* class are learning about report writing and make any necessary adjustments. Figure 6.8 is a map of the informational report genre.

Launching the Learning

- Introduce children to many types of nonfiction writing from a variety of sources—books, periodicals, technology-based resources.
- Set up stations around the room in which children can explore the various subgenres of nonfiction.
- Include nonfiction in the classroom library.
- Teach the text structure of nonfiction to help children understand what they are reading and seeing when exploring nonfiction books.

FIGURE 6.8 Informational Report Genre Map

		Description
Purpose		Demonstrates ability to choose a topic, research it, organize information, and write about the information and data. Selects and uses appropriate nonfiction text features such as charts, graphs, bibliography, table of contents, and appendix.
Characteristics		Has clear organization including sections and section headers. Cites sources. Has guiding question, or inquiry statement, that organizes information. Writing is based on research. Transition words and heading guide writing between the beginning, middle, and end. Supports main ideas with facts and details. Has labels and drawings that represent facts and details.
Uses/ Types		Topic reports All about reports Information articles
Organization		Has clearly developed organization and structure. Structure may be patterned as topic headings, headlines, or topic chapters. Communicates ideas, theories, insights, and information. Has concluding section or sentence. Employs nonfiction conventions including diagrams, charts, table of contents, appendix, and/or bibliography. Presents related information together.
Conventions or Techniques		Show careful reading and understanding of researched topic or content. Variety of sentences develops pacing. Develop context through descriptive and analytical techniques. Exclude extraneous detail. Quote directly from text. Use an organizational technique to research information and track research to create a comprehensive and clear paper. Paraphrase information from research. Track thinking in a logical order. Organize research. Give synopsis of research for context. May include analysis or insights.

- Teach children how to explore nonfiction print sources and find subjects they are passionate about.
- Demonstrate how to gather information.
- Read nonfiction texts out loud to and with children.
- Prepare short choral reading texts from print resources like *Time for Kids* and *Scholastic News*.
- Have children explore books about their favorite topics.
- Fill book baskets with nonfiction resources and texts and place them around the room.
- Point out conventions and features of nonfiction texts.

Figure 6.9 presents examples of teaching charts created at the beginning of an informational report unit of study.

Leading the Learning

- Teach children how reports are organized.
- Teach children how to write a summary.
- Show children how to divide information into sections and create headings.
- Teach and model different ways to begin a report: engaging images and statements, questions, a story or anecdote.
- Define and show examples of nonfiction text features: index, table of contents, headings, diagrams.
- Model writing with details and presenting facts.
- Teach children how to collect information from print sources and then write about what they think, know, and have learned.
- Model four-square report writing (for younger children).
- Model taking notes on index cards and organizing them by topic (for older children).
- Teach children how to check details for accuracy.
- Model removing nebulous words (*it, that, those, he, she*) from reports and adding precise words describing events, actions, people, and things.

Figure 6.10 presents examples of teaching charts used to extend learning in an informational report unit of study.

Writing Outcomes

Expect children to write a short report consisting of a few sentences in kindergarten (see Figure 6.11 and Figure 6.12), create progressively longer and more complex reports in first and second grade (see Figure 6.13 and Figure 6.14), and produce a multiple-paragraph report in third grade.

FIGURE 6.9 Teaching Charts for Informational Report Writing Unit

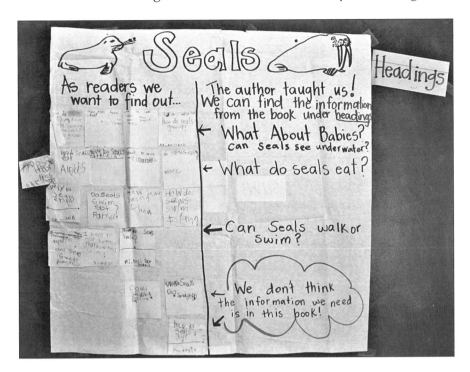

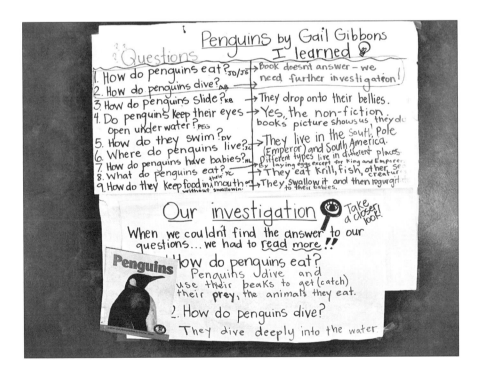

FIGURE 6.9 *(continued)*

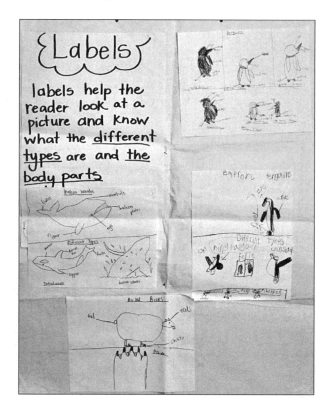

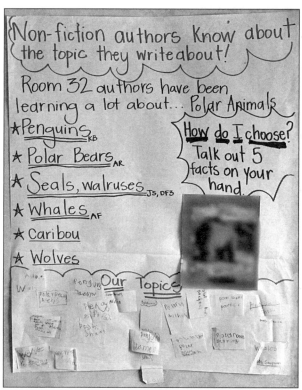

FIGURE 6.10 More Teaching Charts for Informational Report Writing Unit

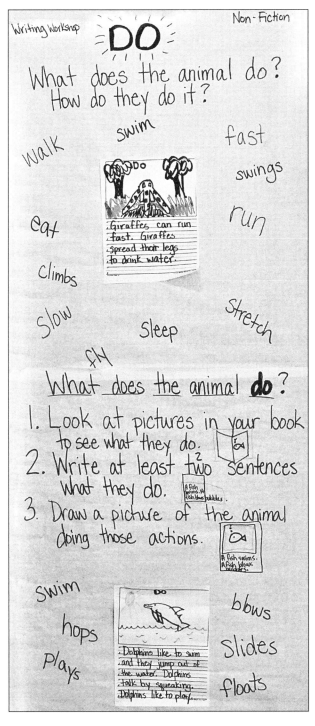

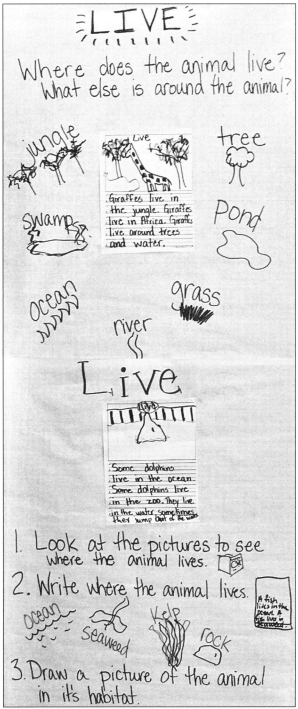

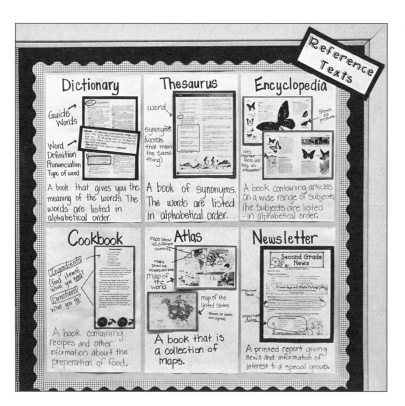

FIGURE 6.10 *(continued)*

FIGURE 6.11 Ali's Rhino Report (Kindergarten)

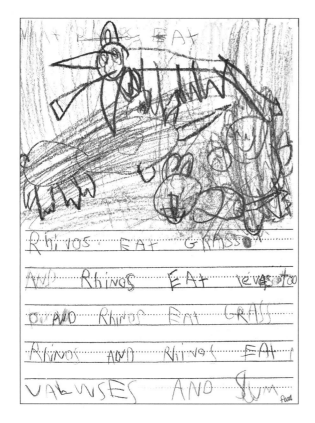

FIGURE 6.12 Yadira's Jaguar Report (Kindergarten)

Yadira

Jaguars Clim Tres.
Jaguars Swim.
Jaguars Fit.
Jagurs hid.
Jagurs slep.
Jagurs hav babe.
Jagurs. yon.

Responses to Literature

In responding to literature, children write about texts that they have read or that have been read to them. Young children usually state whether they liked it or not and why. As children grow as writers, the types of responses become more sophisticated: giving a synopsis; making a statement about the text and supporting it with evidence from the text; making connections to themselves or with other texts.

Children can begin learning to write responses to literature by focusing on their favorite part, what they learned from a story (moral), what they notice is important in the story (theme), and how they connect to the story. Figure 6.15 is a map of the response to literature genre.

FIGURE 6.13 Keylin's Penguin Report (First Grade, four pages of thirteen-page report)

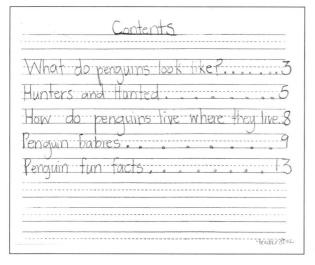

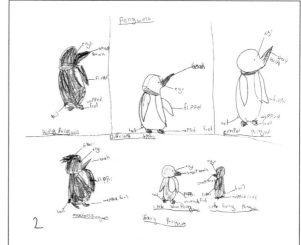

Launching the Learning

■ Read many, many beautiful and thought-provoking picture books to children.

■ Introduce children to different kinds of responses to literature. Find examples in local newspapers and children's magazines.

■ Model writing a response to literature every day. Include poetry, memoirs, and songs.

■ Think out loud when reading a book to the children; stop and tell them what you think about the book and why.

■ Model retelling a favorite story. Have children retell stories to one another and in groups.

■ Write whole-class retellings on large chart paper.

Chapter Six

FIGURE 6.14 Joseph's Shark Report (Second Grade, one text feature from a six-page report)

- Post class-written responses to literature around the room; fill the walls.
- Model providing enough detail from the text so that readers can understand the interpretation.

Figure 6.16 is an example of a teaching chart created at the beginning of a unit of study on responding to literature.

Leading the Learning

- Model retelling and then elaborating on an idea in a piece.
- Compare works by two authors.

FIGURE 6.15 Response to Literature Genre Map

		Description
Purpose of Response		Demonstrates comprehension of literature through interpretation and analysis. Makes a statement about a book or story and provides textual evidence.
Characteristics		Has clear beginning, middle, and end. Identifies the story's theme. Makes a statement, or claim, about the story and provides evidence from the text to support the claim. Includes a brief discussion about the writer's judgment (good or bad) of the book. Book reviews give just enough information to entice a reader to read the book. Answers three basic questions: what is the book about, what is the book's theme or message, is the book worth reading? Presents justification through references to text.
Uses/ Types		Favorite part Literary analysis Book review
Organization		Clearly developed beginning, middle, and end. Beginning may include a summary of the literature. Has engaging beginning to hook the reader. Satisfying ending brings closure to the piece. Includes writer's thoughts and feelings. Presents information chronologically. Focuses on story plot line.
Conventions or Techniques		Show careful reading and understanding of the literature. Focus on story structure and details. Discuss main characters and character actions. Offer opinion about the story. Refer to evidence in the text to back up claims made. Use variety of sentences to develop pacing. Develop context through descriptive techniques. Exclude extraneous detail. Quote directly from text. Paraphrase sections. Retell parts of the text. Give synopsis of story for context. Include analysis.

FIGURE 6.16 Teaching Chart for
Responding to Literature Unit

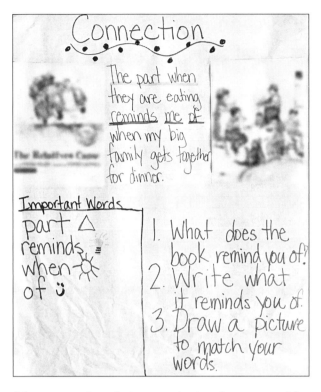

- Model making connections between a text and your own ideas and memories.
- Discuss how stories teach things about life and the world.
- Model writing about what you learned from a story.
- Model writing about what you see as the important ideas in a story.
- Teach children how to support statements and interpretations with evidence in the text.
- Model stating the title and author of the piece you are responding to.
- Teach children how to quote directly from a book.
- Teach children how to write a summary.
- Model summarizing a story and then elaborating on an idea or position.
- Teach children about including a reflective ending in a response to literature; model doing so.

Figure 6.17 presents two examples of teaching charts used to extend learning in a response to literature unit of study.

Writing Outcomes

Kindergartners will write one-page responses—two or three sentences, sometimes more, probably including a picture (it helps them to draw the picture first). They might write about favorite parts of a story or favorite characters; they can use "Favorite Part" writing paper (see the appendix) to help them craft their writing. They may also write about what they learned.

FIGURE 6.17 More Teaching Charts for Responding to Literature Unit

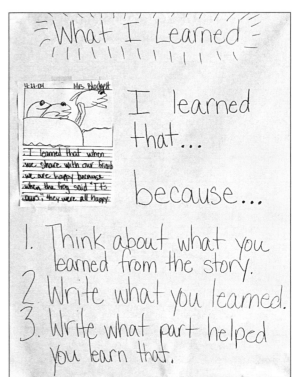

FIGURE 6.18 Robert's Response to Literature (Kindergarten)

FIGURE 6.19 Yadira's Response to Literature (Kindergarten)

(See Figures 6.18 and 6.19.) Children in second and third grade should be writing longer pieces; they need to practice making a statement and then backing up their interpretation with evidence from the text, including quotations. Third graders' responses to literature should be at least two pages long, contain several paragraphs, and be written on appropriate paper (see Figures 6.20 and 6.21).

Letters

I am amazed by how many young children are already sending computer emails and cell phone text messages. Teaching children to communicate with one another informally goes beyond texting! They probably won't be aware of the "ancient" practice of writing and mailing letters unless you call

FIGURE 6.20 Amanda's Response to Literature (Third Grade)

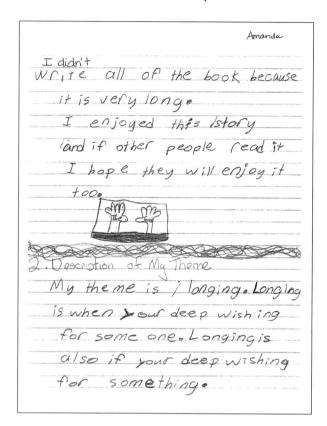

I didn't
write all of the book because
it is very long.
I enjoyed this lstory
and if other people read it
I hope they will enjoy it
too.

2. Description of My Theme.
My theme is / longing. Longing
is when your deep wishing
for some one. Longing is
also if your deep wishing
for something.

My Thoughts And Ideas
I noticed Opel longs so much
for her mom. I feel bad that
Opel only has a dad and not
a mom. I think that is good
that Opel at leist has a
dad and a dog.
I dont even think Opels
mom should com back
because Opels mom drank
And if Opels mom came
back what if she still
drank. I would not like
to have a mom who drank

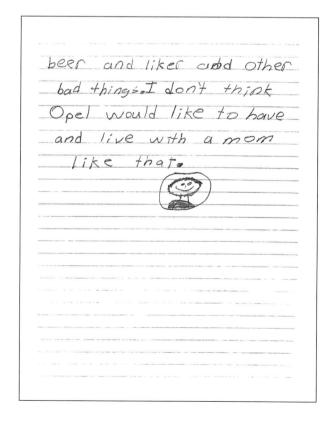

beer and liker and other
bad things. I don't think
Opel would like to have
and live with a mom
like that.

FIGURE 6.21 Kelsey's Response to Literature (Third Grade)

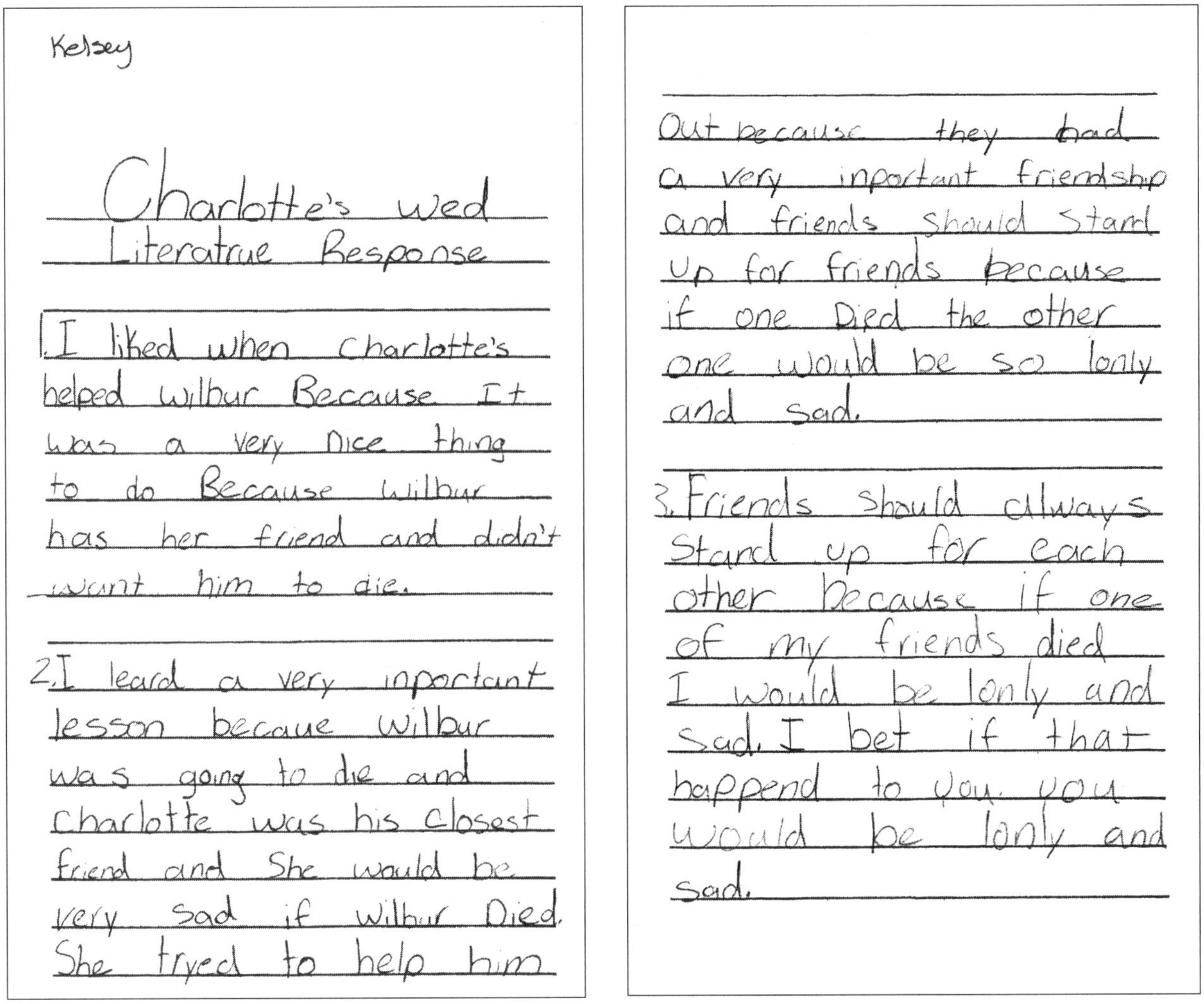

Kelsey

Charlotte's web
Literatrue Response

1. I liked when Charlotte's helped Wilbur Because It was a very nice thing to do Because Wilbur has her friend and didn't want him to die.

2. I leard a very inportant lesson becaue wilbur was going to die and Charlotte was his closest friend and She would be very sad if wilbur Died. She tryed to help him

Out because they had a very inportant friendshp and friends should Stand Up for friends because if one Died the other one would be so lonly and sad.

3. Friends should always Stand up for each other because if one of my friends died I would be lonly and sad. I bet if that happend to you. you would be lonly and sad.

their attention to it and celebrate the virtues of sending letters written from the heart and receiving letters that feel personal and connective. Young children first learn that letter writing is a fun way to communicate with others that has a form, function, and discourse separate from ultra-informal emails and text messages. As they grow older, they learn that letters are a formal way to accomplish and document formal actions and activities.

Letter writing is often brushed aside as an easy form to master, one that doesn't require much attention in our teaching. This isn't true. Writing sophisticated, formal letters still give me pause. Figure 6.22 is a map for the letter-writing genre.

Launching the Learning

■ Introduce the purposes of letter writing.
■ Bring in lots of different examples: junk mail solicitations, personal letters, letters to the editor in a newspaper, Dear Abby–type letters asking

FIGURE 6.22 Letter-Writing Genre Map

	Description
Purpose of Letters	Shares ideas with a specific audience through a written communication.
Characteristics	Letters of request require clear identification of key questions and issues. Employs a polite tone. Connects with people in a professional tone, or a personal tone. Follows a format including an opening, salutation, body, and closing. Types of letters follow a specific format.
Uses/Types	Personal Business Request Notes Cards Invitations Email
Organization	Heading Inside address Salutation/greeting Body Closing Signature First paragraph identifies author and purpose of letter. Middle paragraphs identify what is requested or communicated. Last paragraph summarizes information and includes a brief thank-you statement.
Conventions or Techniques	Include details to describe issue, information, or request. Succinctly address issue. Clearly state specific information (invitation). Write with a specific purpose in mind, to accomplish a task. Write in conversational tone (friendly letter). Write in professional tone (business letter).

for advice in a public forum, cover letters for manuscript submissions and résumés.
- Post letters on the writing workshop learning board.
- Write class letters to people in the school: another class, the lunch ladies, the principal, the librarian, the school secretary.

- Demonstrate the letter-writing format: salutation and closing.
- Brainstorm letter-writing purposes and topics.
- Discuss appropriate letter-writing punctuation

Figure 6.23 presents examples of teaching charts created at the beginning of a letter-writing unit of study. (Also see Figures 3.13 and 3.14)

Leading the Learning

- Teach students how letters are organized.
- Demonstrate adding details to a personal letter, then have the children write to classmates, other schoolmates, family members, or friends.
- Demonstrate adding details to a business letter, then have the class write to the principal, the librarian, or businesspeople in the community.
- Teach children how to capture an anecdote in a letter or relate important facts to help the letter recipient understand the point they want to make.

FIGURE 6.23 Teaching Charts for Letter-Writing Unit

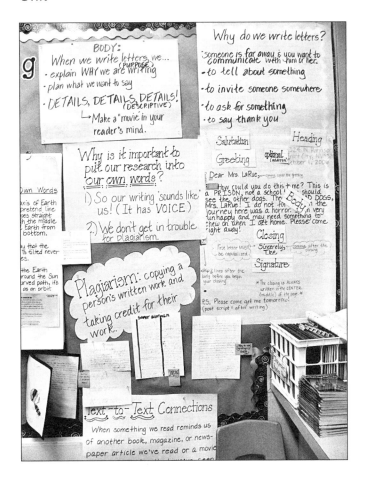

- Model stating a fact in a business letter; show examples of real letters (requesting playground equipment, complaining about lunch lines and school cafeteria food choices, telling parents about grade-level book lists, etc.).

Writing Outcomes

In kindergarten and first grade, all children can write short personal letters (see Figures 6.24 and 6.25). Second and third graders should be able to write a short informational letter on a specific topic to a school official or other person. Third graders should be able to write personal letters on appropriate paper that are at least two pages long and make a specific point (for example, a letter to their second-grade teacher telling her they liked the way she read aloud to them and a specific incident or event they remember from the previous year).

Procedural Writing

Procedural writing is important in our everyday lives. We read instruction books, recipes, technology troubleshooting guides, and manuals that come with our cars and major appliances. We read directions for renewing our motor vehicle licenses, getting money from an automatic teller, and order-

FIGURE 6.24 Dariah's Letter (Kindergarten)   **FIGURE 6.25** Damon's Letter (Kindergarten)

ing books online. We read directions everywhere, every day, including those on parking meters! Children will apply the ability to write procedures in science and math classes as they get older. They will also use procedural writing every day as they work and run households. Young children learn procedural writing by focusing on steps and logic. Help them see that their writing needs to be in a logical order, explicit, and clear. Figure 6.26 is a map of the procedural writing genre.

FIGURE 6.26   Procedural Writing Genre Map

		Description
	Purpose of Procedural Writing	Provides an explanation. Describes how to make something, how to complete a task, how something works, how to get somewhere.
Characteristics		Clear and concise. In a logical order. Easy to follow. Avoids jargon language.
Uses/Types		How-to directions Recipes Annotated map directions Computer manuals Appliance manuals Learn to . . . books (knit a sweater, play the piano) Craft magazines
Organization		Beginning identifies topic. Middle includes a set of instructions. Order of events or steps is organized by time, location, and need. Steps are in logical order beginning with first step and concluding with last step. Middle steps include clear description of action and directions. Clear outcomes described at end.
Conventions or Techniques		Use description to guide reader to visualize each step to make it real. Use sensory details in description to make each step vivid and easy to follow. Use simple, easy-to-follow language. Avoid flowery language and jargon. Revise action to make ideas clear. Follow a time line. Use subheadings and bulleted lists to provide detailed explanation.

Launching the Learning

- Teach children the purposes of procedural writing.
- Bring in various types of procedural writing, including recipes and instruction manuals.
- Create teaching charts that unpack the thinking in the procedural writing.
- Use language to engage the children in the unpacking process ("The author tells us to . . ."; "Step six says . . .").
- Teach how-to writing.
- Have the class generate how-to pieces (how to jump rope, how to wash our hands, how to line up for recess) and reenact the procedures to ensure steps aren't missing.
- Brainstorm steps in a process; list the steps in order.
- Model drawing a how-to illustration and then writing a how-to piece.

Figure 6.27 presents two examples of teaching charts created at the beginning of a procedural writing unit of study.

Leading the Learning

- Teach children to develop a list of how-to topics.
- Model thinking through the steps to complete a task.
- Teach children the structure of procedural writing.
- Create teaching charts listing procedural and how-to writing vocabulary.

FIGURE 6.27 Teaching Charts for Procedural-Writing Unit

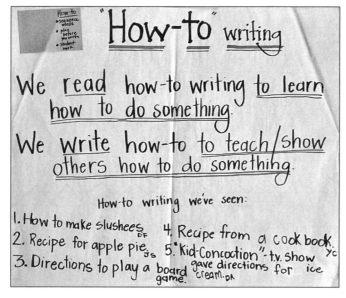 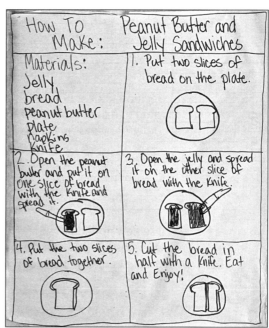

FIGURE 6.28 More Teaching Charts for Procedural-Writing Unit

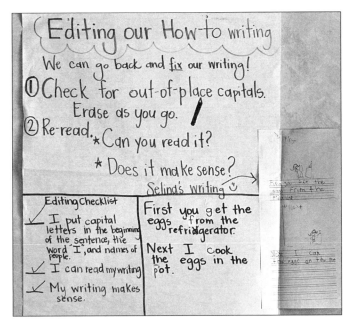

- Model using how-to writing vocabulary appropriately—*first, next, then, last; first, second, third, fourth.*
- Model using a number or letter outline to organize steps in a process (in a recipe, for example).
- Teach children to add details and revise for clarity.
- Teach children how to put the steps in a process into logical order.
- Show children how to draw pictures that match the written steps.

Figure 6.28 presents examples of teaching charts used to extend learning in a procedural writing unit of study.

Writing Outcomes

Children in kindergarten may begin by drawing a how-to piece and then adding a single word to each frame. By the end of the year, they should be writing simple sentences denoting the steps in a process (see Figure 6.29). First graders should write clearer steps and match them with a picture of the appropriate action. Second and third graders may still be writing simple procedures, but their choice of topics will be more sophisticated—how to

FIGURE 6.29 "How to Ride My Bike," by Yadira (Kindergarten, first few pages of student project)

help their dad wash the car, how to make enchiladas, how to cook sticky rice (see Figure 6.30). Third graders might even tell how to complete an Internet search or how to use the computer to create a digital scrapbook. They have a multitude of experiences to call upon, so make sure you set your expectations high enough.

Poetry

Learning about poetry is a sensory and emotional experience that leads children to look at and see things from a new perspective. Lucy Calkins and Stephanie Parsons (2003) call poetry "powerful writing in tiny packages," and that's exactly what it is. If you feel you cannot *teach* children how to write poetry because you don't *write* poetry, let go of that idea and give it a try. Your students will blossom as writers who can see things in the world from various perspectives, they will grow in their ability to think, and they will begin to write with more description and detail. Yes, you'll need to write poetry to use in your teaching charts, but it needn't be worthy of a Pulitzer. It just needs to reflect you, show your students that you are a

FIGURE 6.29 "How to Ride My Bike," by Yadira (Kindergarten, first few pages of student project) *(continued)*

Thin I git My haimit

Thin I go fast

4

learner along with them, and illustrate that poets come in all shapes, sizes, and abilities. Your model needs only to reflect the objective you are teaching that day: description, powerful words, line breaks, perspective. It doesn't have to rhyme, it doesn't have to be funny, it only needs to engage you. The children will be engaged and enthralled because you are writing with them. Figure 6.31 is a map of the poetry genre.

Launching the Learning

- Introduce children to many poems written by many authors.
- Read poems every day; vary when you do it.
- Post poems around the room.
- Point out the different structures of poems.
- Discuss differences between rhyming poems and poems that do not rhyme.
- Teach children to look at objects and people deeply.
- Begin by teaching children to look at objects from a new perspective

FIGURE 6.30 "How to Make a Star Out of a Necklace," by Roselle (Second Grade)

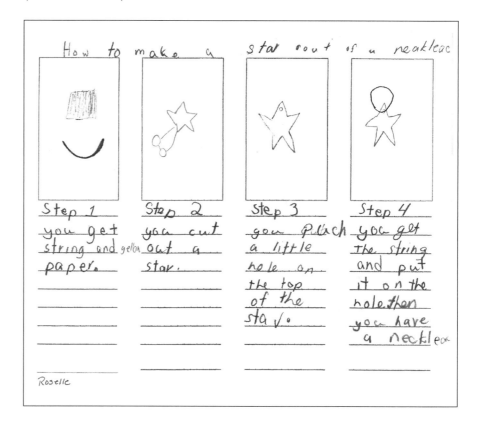

How to make a star oout of a neakleac

Step 1
you get
string and gelon
paper.

Step 2
you cut
out a
star.

step 3
you punch
a little
hole on
the top
of the
star.

Step 4
you get
the string
and put
it on the
hole. then
you have
a necklea

Roselle

rather than in terms of the shape, color, or use they're usually associated with.

■ Teach children to notice (respectfully) details about people: color of hair and eyes, type of hairstyle, body differences (short, tall, etc.), personalities.
■ Model writing about things you see, hear, and feel.
■ Introduce children to various poetry structures.
■ Take children on an outdoor walking tour and have them look at things in the world and notice the details. Then have them write about these things and details.

Figure 6.32 presents examples of teaching charts created at the beginning of a poetry unit of study.

Leading the Learning

■ Discuss how objects can represent ideas, feelings, and thoughts.
■ Discuss how things and actions represent our relationships with people: ring = love or marriage; going to the fair = relationship with a grandparent who annually makes the trip; apple picking = making apple pie with Mom each fall; tamales = Christmas family gatherings.

FIGURE 6.31   Poetry Genre Map

		Description
Purpose of Poems		Authentic and individual expression of an idea, thought, experience, or feeling using few words.
Characteristics		Captures vivid images in a few words to express the author's thoughts and feelings. Poetry paints pictures with words. Poetry speaks to the soul and from the soul. Sounds different than prose. Written in lines and groups of lines, or stanzas. Some poems use regular rhyme or rhythm. Free-verse poetry does not use regular rhythm. Focuses on details; visual, sensory. Uses imagery focused on specific memory, feeling, idea, thought, or experience.
Uses/Types		Cinquain Limerick Free verse Lyrics Sonnet Haiku Couplet
Organization		The length and placement of each line affect the poem's meaning. The lines form a meaningful whole. The idea is creatively developed and presented. Meaning deepens throughout the poem. Line breaks enhance meaning and effect.
Conventions or Techniques		Use figures of speech: simile, metaphor, personification, hyperbole. Employ the sound of poetry: alliteration, end rhyme, internal rhyme, onomatopoeia, repetition, rhythm. Overall techniques: engaging voice, beautiful language, fluid movement from line to line, consistent voice. Can focus on theme or form. Structure and elements are unlimited and should focus on conveying author's meaning.

FIGURE 6.32   Teaching Charts for Poetry Unit

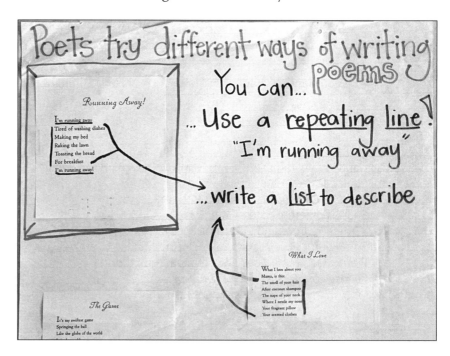

FIGURE 6.33   More Teaching Charts for Poetry Unit

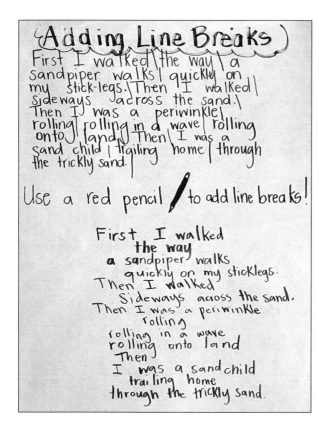

- Model writing about these representations.
- Begin by having children write memory moments.
- Model taking a memory moment and circling powerful words in the piece that get at the big idea, or meaning. Rewrite these powerful words on a separate paper. Model reading the words, thinking of the moment, and then writing a poem.
- Teach children how to make an analogy and write it down.
- Teach children how to notice details in objects and actions and write a poem about the details they've noticed.
- Teach children about line breaks and arranging lines on a page.
- Model descriptive writing.

Figure 6.33 presents examples of teaching charts used to extend learning in a poetry unit of study.

Writing Outcomes

All children can write poetry. Poems don't necessarily become longer as children develop as writers, but they do become more thoughtful, have more depth, and use more sophisticated conventions. Encourage your students to write poetry and give poems as gifts to friends and family. You could assemble a book of poems written by class members and let each child take home a copy to share with loved ones.

Destiny Rios' Poetry (First Grade)

Crystal

When the snow comes
it's a crystal going
with the snow
falling,
falling,
when
the
snow rains
the snow crystal is
beautiful
and sweet.

Denise Villa's Poetry (First Grade)

The Sky

When it rains
some little
blue comes with the rain.
And with the sun

comes some
little yellow, comes
with some
little blue and with yellow too.
When the cold comes
some white
comes too.

Keylin Bejar Torres' Poetry (First Grade)

The Grass

The grass,
   makes me,
   loved,
   because it,
   reminds me,
   of my,
   mom's hair.
It,
   makes me,
   loved,
   because,
   my mom,
   loves me
   and even,
   if she
   yells at,
   me
   I still,
   love her,
   and even,
   if she's,
   mad at me,
   and even,
   if she
   grounds me.
   I still,
   love her.
and that,
   means,
   that she,
   loves me,
   too,
   and that's

what makes,
me loved.
and all,
of the grass,
curly and
orange and brown,
reminds me,
of her hair
because I,
love her.

Familiarity With Genres Is Not Enough

Dear Mommy,

I am worried about school. It is new. Please go with me on the first day. I love you.
Love,
Sayeh

My daughter wrote me this letter when she was very young. She understood, at the tender age of six, that she could communicate with me in an intimate, connective way that only she and I were privy to. She knew the letter-writing basics; she understood purpose, form, and simple organization. While she knew these things, they weren't enough to help her become the writer she needed to be in third grade, fourth grade, and beyond.

Craft

First, Sayeh needed to learn about the craft of writing. Here, expect the unexpected. Children will develop abilities you may have thought they were incapable of. *All* children, not just some or those who arrive in your classroom in September with well-developed language abilities, will learn to write well. As you teach writing, children's vocabulary and their ability to use and manipulate language will grow. As you teach writing strategies, your students will practice them and come to own them. Strategies especially important for young children to know and be able to use include these:

- writing descriptively
- writing with a unique voice
- setting up an organizational structure
- establishing tension
- developing characters
- creating settings
- introducing literary language

Strategies and craft are used in any and all genres and help children write with depth and joy and playfulness. When we teach craft and writing strategies, we are teaching children to be thoughtful about what real writers do. We have them imitate these strategies at first, try them on for size; in time, they make them their own. Go back to Figure 6.7 and look at how Roselle used literary language in her narrative. I can still hear her big laugh and see her satisfied grin after she finished reading this piece to me. She didn't know about wondrous and beautiful language when she started second grade, but she learned how writers write, learned to play with language, and was able to add beautiful and wondrous words to her own writing.

Conventions

Students need specific and direct instruction about more than content. They also need to focus on the conventions: vocabulary, grammar, and spelling. Children's vocabularies will grow in size and richness as they borrow words they hear and read and gradually make them part of who they are and how they think and talk.

Children's ability to spell will increase as they apply the print-sound code to increasingly difficult words. They will begin spelling frequently used words and simple consonant-vowel-consonant patterns automatically, and they'll gradually learn to spell words that contain more difficult patterns. Children can write before they can spell. The four examples of kindergartners' writing in Figure 6.34 show the progression from scribble writing to sounding out words.

Young children begin by scribbling, then produce strings of letters representing sounds, then spell words phonetically, and finally are able to spell them conventionally. The key is to encourage this developmental progress, not hamper it by making children feel that they can't write or spell. Invented spelling helps children learn to apply phonics strategies as they construct words by thinking about letter-sound relationships. By allowing children to spell words in the way they hear them, we strengthen their conceptual understanding of spelling patterns rather than force them to rely on memorization (Spandel 2008). Of course, children can't spell words only by sounding them out; you need to teach a variety of word patterns and phonetic constructions as well. Remember, too, that good readers are better spellers and use a greater variety of spelling strategies when writing (Tompkins 1997). Have appropriate expectations, include spelling mini-lessons in your curriculum, but make your writing workshop about communicating, *not* about spelling.

To guide your instruction in spelling and conventions, refer to expectations in your state's or district's curriculum frameworks and content standards. When working with kindergartners or first graders who are just developing print skills, create a context for their work, simplify the task, and avoid detours (Clay 2001). Following are some ways to do this:

FIGURE 6.34   Children's Spelling Development
Progresses Over Time

- Teach them to tell and write memory moments.
- Encourage them to get their ideas on paper by first drawing, then writing.
- Celebrate their writing and the fact that they can share it with someone.
- Allow them to spell words as they hear them.
- Set up word walls they can use to spell frequently used words.
- Teach conventions appropriately (just periods and capital letters when they initially record their ideas on paper).
- Teach the writer, not the writing.

Children need lots of practice in order to internalize high-frequency words. Displaying these on a word wall or making them part of a word bank helps young children develop a fluid vocabulary. Have the class sing and chant words, poems, songs, and sentences. Introduce new words each week by displaying them on a small chart and asking children to look at each word, say it, sing it, and vocally stretch out the letters as they spell it.

Your students will move from writing in the casual, shorthand way they speak to writing with voice and literary language. They learn the language of authors by reading a lot, writing a lot, and learning to read like a writer.

Thoughts in Conclusion

When I ask children what makes good writing, they usually tell me periods and capital letters. When I ask teachers what makes good writing, they usually tell me punctuation and capitalization. It's true that children need to learn the rules of appropriate punctuation, but you need to teach these rules as appropriate to the grade level and in context. Children must never get the impression that perfect writing is well punctuated and nothing else. Teach them that good writing is well punctuated *after* revision and editing, and then teach them the rules you want them to apply *during* revision and editing. Teach them the rules, but also teach them to break these rules in the name of style and vigorous, memorable communication. This comes about with lots of practice and with lots of coaching from you.

CHAPTER SEVEN

Knowing How to Help
Intervention for Struggling Writers

I see her now. She's sitting in the corner, staring quietly at her writing, which is clipped to a board propped on her knees. Her eyes glisten, as if big tears are about to slip out and roll down her cheeks. The other children don't notice her; they are busy writing, immersed in their own thinking, working feverishly to get their fleeting thoughts on paper before they forget. But there she sits, wiping her nose on her pink jacket. Her pencil lies in her open hand, one finger slightly curled around the eraser. When the tears finally come, she tips her head forward, resting it on her knees so no one can see.

She is struggling to write. Day after day she begins writing with the hope and expectation that today she'll be able to unscramble the words, put her story down on paper the way she hears it in her mind.

I walk up to her and put my arm around her shoulders. Her writing folder is open on the floor beside her, filled with papers that have one or two words written on them in print that looks cramped and shaky. "Come with me; we're going to draw today. I know you can tell me your story in pictures." I gently take her elbow and help her to her feet. She follows me, a little sad cloud, and sits down at the teaching table, on which I have placed a stack of plain white paper and a set of crayons. "Go ahead, draw your picture." She smiles weakly and begins.

I wonder if she *can* draw her story, this young writer who is so frustrated and unhappy. Normally children's writing folders tell me a lot about what they know as writers, but hers contains too little writing to make a valid assessment. I know that watching her draw will tell me a bit more about her abilities. But before I can come up with a different way to teach her, I have to assess what she needs to learn.

Understanding Your Students' Gifts and Needs

Children know so much more than we realize. The key is to unlock their potential by showing them specifically how to do the things that are tripping them up. Even the child you're convinced will never learn to write can write. You just need to know which doors to open.

Focus on how your young students are developing as writers. Children develop as writers in a variety of ways, but focusing your teaching on three main areas will help you provide precise intervention lessons:

- writing process
- writing craft
- writing conventions

Writing Process

The writing process comprises five actions: developing ideas, drafting, revising and refining, editing (for syntax, spelling, and conventions), and publishing. In assessing what children know and are able to do in each of these areas, you'll also evaluate their writing habits, daily output, the ease with which they write, how regularly they reread their own work, and how they respond to the work of their peers (August and Vockley 2002). A final factor to consider is their ability to monitor the construction of their own text (Clay 2001).

Writing Craft

Understanding and applying craft means understanding genre components and structures. Children need to know what makes a genre a genre and be able to use the appropriate text structure correctly when writing in a given genre. They should also be able to use literary language and vocabulary appropriate to the genre. A guide to different genres appears in Chapter 6.

Writing Conventions

Writing conventions consist primarily of punctuation, grammar, and spelling. Children begin learning simple conventions and move along a continuum until they can use sophisticated conventions appropriate to the genre they are writing in and explain their reason for doing so (and ignore these conventions when the occasion calls for it).

Intervention Activities and Lessons

You've observed a child in your class who doesn't—or won't—write. You've assessed the child's abilities and needs and see places to intervene, provide a learning on-ramp, so the child can begin writing and feel successful. What do you do? What can you do? Following are a few suggestions.

Reteaching Charts

Reflect on whether your whole-group minilessons have been explicit enough to help the children who need a bit more time or another explanation in order to understand. Then use these minilessons as springboards to plan small-group strategy lessons in which you reteach the lessons and create small

FIGURE 7.1 A Teaching Chart from Small-Group Teaching

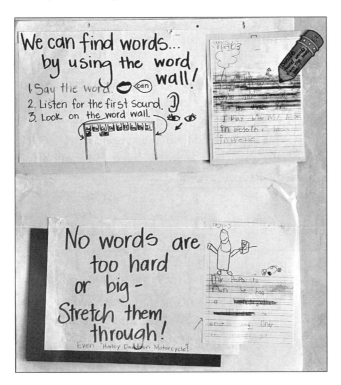

charts to reinforce the learning (an example chart is shown in Figure 7.1). Or have the children create the charts themselves, in their own words.

Writing Across Your Fingers

Teach children to use their fingers to tell their stories, lock in their small moments, or remember information for their reports. First, ask a child to think of what he wants to write about—to visualize the story, event, or information in his mind. Then have him talk it through out loud, using his fingers to itemize each separate element. When he goes off to write, his fingers will remind him what he wants to write, in what order.

"Me" Writing

Children who move around a lot may need to make connections with more parts of their bodies than just their fingers to help them remember what to write. This technique works especially well when children are writing memory moments, or personal narratives. Have the child point to the corresponding parts of her body while she rehearses her story mentally or orally; she can then use these body parts to jog her memory while she is writing. For example:

- *Head*: What's my idea for a memory moment?
- *Eyes, nose, mouth, ears*: What did I see, smell, taste, say, or hear?

- *Hands*: What did I touch or do?
- *Body*: What did I wear? How did I move about?
- *Feet*: Where did I go? Where did others go?

Favorite Words

Looking at words can help children begin writing. Give them a special sheet (see the example in Figure 7.2) on which they can record favorite words and which they can then look at to get their writing juices flowing (Akhavan 2007). You can write the children's favorite words on the sheet, or the children can write them themselves (just make sure doing it isn't frustrating). Model browsing your own favorite-words sheet and thinking of ideas and memorable moments to write about.

FIGURE 7.2   My Favorite Word Bank Sheet

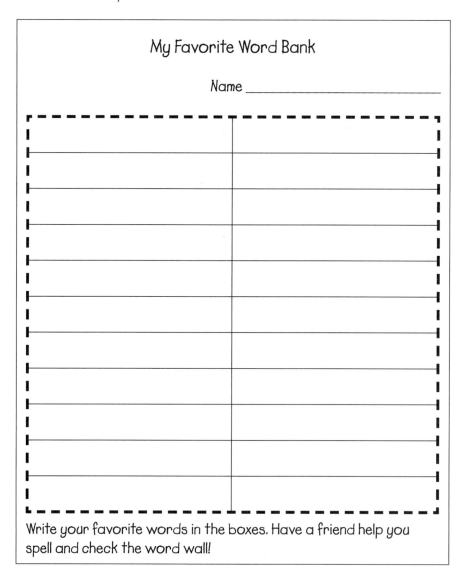

Chapter Seven

FIGURE 7.3 Words I Use Sheet

Words I Use

Name _____

My Spelling	Word Wall Spelling

Write your favorite words in the boxes. Have a friend help you spell and check by using the word wall!

Words I Have Trouble Spelling

Give children a sheet on which they can record words they use a lot but have trouble remembering how to spell (see Figure 7.3). They can copy the correct spelling of the words from the word wall or other forms of word banks in the classroom. Then, when they get stuck spelling one of these common words, they can check this sheet. The list of one hundred most frequently used words in the appendix includes more than half the words children are likely to use in their writing (Fry and Kress 2006).

Sound-Spelling Card

When children have trouble remembering which letters represent which sounds, use a sound-spelling card. Use a sound-spelling card available in your literacy series or in a teaching resource. One excellent sound-spelling card is available in *Guided Reading,* by Fountas and Pinnell (1996). Copy the card on sturdy paper and have children keep it in their writing folder, so they can use it to match letters and sounds. (Children shouldn't overrely on this scaffold; you want them to internalize the connections between letters and sounds as quickly as possible.)

Bubblegum Stretch

Many children immediately rush over to you or a friend, breathlessly asking, "How do you spell such and so?" They need to learn to slow down, to stretch out the sounds in the word so they can think about the letters associated with those sounds and thus attempt to spell the word on their own (Fountas and Pinnell 1996, 2006).

Get children to practice stretching out sounds, listening to them, and writing down the letters that represent the sounds (Bear et al. 1996). (A stretch-to-spell teaching chart is shown in Figure 7.4.) If you think accompanying this vocalization with a physical action will help a student, have him put his thumb and forefinger on his lips, then pull the word from his mouth as he says it, as if he were stretching out a piece of bubble gum. (A blackline master for a card reminding students to do the bubblegum stretch is included in the appendix.)

FIGURE 7.4   Stretch-to-Spell Teaching Chart

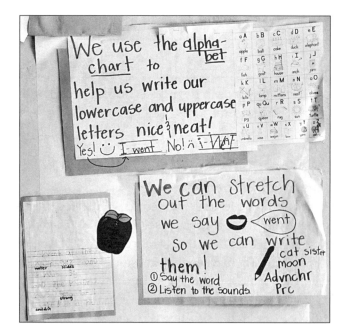

This strategy also helps children who get stuck because they don't have the self-confidence to spell words with temporary spelling. Accept *any* approximation of the word in the beginning to help build children's self-confidence.

Elkonian Boxes

Children who have trouble hearing the sounds in words need to increase their phonemic awareness. Elkonian boxes, also known as sound boxes, can help them (see Figure 7.5). These boxes are a series of squares, one for every phoneme (sound, not letter) in a word (Clay 2001; Tompkins 2007). The child says the word, placing a manipulative, like a penny or a paper clip, in each successive box as she says each sound—beginning sound, medial sounds, ending sound. A blackline master is in the Appendix.

A child using Elkonian boxes to help him hear the sounds in *dog*, for example, would say /d/ and push a penny into the first box, say /ŏ/ and push a second penny into the middle box, and say /g/ and push a third penny into the last box.

Remember to use the appropriate number of boxes for each *sound* in a word, not each letter.

FIGURE 7.5   Elkonian Box

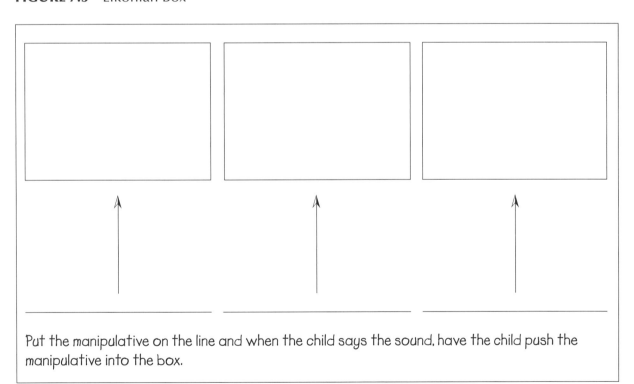

Put the manipulative on the line and when the child says the sound, have the child push the manipulative into the box.

CHAPTER EIGHT

Language Sense
Helping English Learners Write

Even though I have years of experience working with children learning English, I sometimes feel paralyzed when faced with helping English learners write. Thankfully, this paralysis lasts only long enough for me to regroup after something in the classroom has thrown me off balance.

These moments of uncertainty usually occur when I am partner-teaching a writing workshop and have just finished the minilesson. "Go off and write," I say, and the children do just that. Then, while I am moving about the room conferring with children, reteaching and redirecting, I notice two or three children sitting and waiting, or I hear the rapid translation of directions, as a more fluent child tries to explain to the child learning English what she should be doing.

I should know better. It isn't appropriate to teach a minilesson to children who are learning English in the same way you teach a minilesson to children whose first language is English. It also isn't appropriate to tell children learning English to *go off and write* and expect them to be successful without giving them more support. Knowing what to do to support these children's acquisition of English is important.

Supporting English Learners in Writing Workshop

Children who are learning English acquire language by participating in the writing workshop (Krashen 2003; Samway 2006). Don't wait until children reach a specific level of oral language proficiency before teaching them writing. Children learning English can draw, label, watch other children write, and confer with peers about writing and by doing so acquire language and develop important academic writing experiences.

Scaffold your minilessons so that English learners aren't sitting there bored, watching you model and create a teaching chart and wondering what in the world is going on (Freeman and Freeman 1998). Slow down; pause often while speaking to allow children time to process what you are saying; and use lots of visuals (Rea and Mercuri 2007; Strickland 1998).

Give English learners ways other than drawing to participate in independent writing; help them begin to label words or experiment with temporary spelling. As they begin to gain a little English proficiency, don't let them get stuck writing the same thing over and over again; help them develop their ability to control new writing strategies or processes.

When implementing scaffolds to support English learners, focus on helping the children understand, interact, communicate, and learn. There aren't any specific magic scaffolds; use whichever ones work, and embed them in your regular classroom routines (Peregoy and Boyle 1999). Some of the scaffolds I suggest in this chapter further language acquisition and development. Others are specific, direct interventions to help a child learn (Maria 1998). Still others outline appropriate materials to use as models for young English learners attempting to write in this new language.

Songs and Poetry

Sing to your students! Read poetry aloud. Let the children hear English, feel English, and move to English. Helping them develop an ear for the rhythm of the well-crafted phrases in songs and poetry is the best way to help children prepare to write. Before they are able to remember words and names and labels for things, children will respond to the emotion conveyed by the rhythmic lilt of your voice (Ball 2006). Fun poems help children learn without realizing it.

Leaves and Water

When you
put a
leaf in
the water
it floats
   floats
   floats
   softly
   away.
—Yessenia

The butterfly wings
sound like a slow fan
blowing around
my ears.
—Yessenia

Post poems and song lyrics on charts (or type them out and display them using your computer and an LCD projector) and read them often while pointing to each word with a pointer. Decorate the posters with

FIGURE 8.1 Examples of Picture-Word Cards

Picture Word Card

Write the word in the box and then draw a picture to match the word.

Picture	Word

Picture	Word

pictures to help the children remember what the words mean. Let a child be the leader and point to each word as the class recites together.

In her narrative piece (see Figure 6.7), third grader Roselle borrowed language from books she had heard read aloud. Once she acquired some facility with English, the words she had stored up inside came spilling forth. Roselle had many experiences reading poems and reciting poems aloud.

Writing Buddies

Don't expect English learners to write alone; pair them with another child who has acquired more English or who speaks English as a first language. Begin by making writing a group activity. Share the pen with the whole class every day and create a piece of interactive writing. As children become familiar with stretching to spell, thinking of their messages, and writing them down, have them attempt the process with a writing buddy.

Deliberately choose who will work together (and post the writing buddy chart on the wall so children can refer to it). You may want to have a more proficient child work with a child new to English. You can also have two English learners work together once they have acquired some English, particularly if they speak the same first language. This way, they can support one another and talk in their first language as they make sure what they need to do in English.

Picture-Word Cards

Picture-word cards (see Figure 8.1) help children expand their vocabularies. They can use the cards at home to practice new words or go over them with a writing buddy. Larger cards (at least three inches by five inches) are best for small hands to manipulate and allow the picture and the word to appear side by side. (A template is included in the appendix.) Type or write a word on the right side of the card and put a picture on the left side of the card. Use the Internet: google the image you need, print it out, and paste it on the card. Be careful to not download or copy images that have a copyright line or are copyright protected.

Toy Stories

Children new to English may need to manipulate real items to help them learn vocabulary and feel comfortable speaking aloud. Toy stories help children rehearse a narrative orally and give them opportunities to learn the names of objects. Collect a variety of small plastic toys, like those found in discount stores—character figures, food, animals, dollhouse furniture, almost anything works well. Model telling a story by touching the toys and saying the words. For example:

Story	Action
I	Point to yourself.
sat	Make motion of sitting.
in a	Pick up a toy chair.
chair.	Place the toy chair on the table or work surface in front of you and point to it.

Add to the story using other toy items; pick up a toy hot dog as you tell about eating a hot dog, for example. The possibilities are endless.

Children learning English need to work with a partner who knows the names of some of the objects. Or have children practice the names of a few objects first before telling stories to one another.

Picture-Word Banks

Run off, on sturdy paper, several copies of the blackline master (see Figure 8.2). (A template is included in the appendix.) Type or write selected words on the right side of each rectangle and paste a picture on the left side. (Or have children draw pictures to match the words on the sheet.) Then have children keep these cards in their writing folders.

Picture-word banks are very helpful to children who have acquired some English but still need help remembering words and using them in their writing. They are able to see and recall many words at a glance.

Dialogue Journals

Create dialogue journals by gathering a few pieces of paper underneath a construction paper cover, or purchase small notebooks. Use these journals as a place in which you and your English learners write back and forth to each other. Your students have a real reason to write (a letter to you!), and you model using the English language and offer lots of encouragement.

Dialogue journals are a safe way for students to explore language and make the mistakes that inevitably result. Encourage your English learners to write freely and without hesitation (which is not easy for them to do) and

FIGURE 8.2 Picture-Word Bank

Picture Word Bank

Name ____________________

Word	Picture
Word	Picture
Word	Picture
Word	Picture
Word	Picture

then praise them in your responses. Never, ever cross out what a child has written and correct it! Instead, model the correct locutions in the sentences you write back to her.

Sentence Cards

Sentence cards help English learners who have learned a bit of English but cannot yet do more than label pictures when writing alone jump-start their writing. In this activity, you sit with a child and help him practice building sentences.

Write various verbs, nouns, and pronouns on index cards, preferably words the child is familiar with. Then create simple sentences the student can act out using his own body or a small toy. For example, you might use two cards to build the sentence *I jump*. After you build the sentence, the child can act it out by jumping, then look at the words on the cards and write the sentence on a whiteboard or a piece of paper. Or build various *I like _____* sentences (*I like ice cream*, for example) using small toys that represent things the child likes. Then the child can say and write the sentences.

After children have more confidence with writing in English, encourage them to create related sentences without using sentence cards. For example, if a child builds the sentence *I like ice cream* using cards, encourage her to write a similar sentence that includes an adjective: *I like chocolate ice cream*. See Figure 8.3 for an example of sentence card sentences.

Using sentence cards, children can "write" without worrying about how to spell words in English. It's a game that builds their confidence before they start writing on blank pages.

FIGURE 8.3   Sentence Card Sentences

Sentence-Strip Stories

Sentence-strip stories are extensions of sentence cards. You'll need sentence strips and a pocket chart (or a tape dispenser). A pocket chart lets you reorder sentences easily, but taping sentence strips to a wall or whiteboard works fine as well.

Working with children individually or in a small group, brainstorm a memory moment, perhaps something they do every day at school. Write the story down as they tell it, placing each sentence on a separate strip of paper. (Children learning English are usually not verbose; a sentence will likely fit on a single strip.) Then insert the sentence strips into the pocket chart. Prompt the children to add more details to the story about what the characters did. As you create more sentence strips, insert them into the pocket chart in the correct order (see Figure 8.4), moving the sentences that are already there as necessary. Finally, read the group story aloud together.

This activity lets children practice some of the writing strategies you are teaching in the minilessons without actually writing. The children are writing orally, telling the story to you and then thinking about where to add details.

FIGURE 8.4   Sentence-Strip Story Example

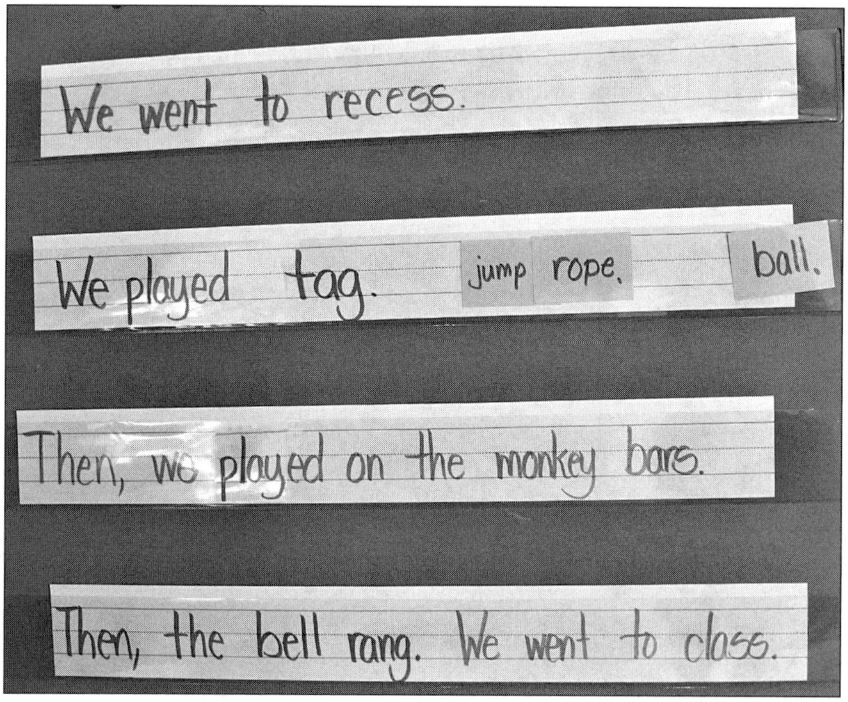

Four-Square Writing

Four-square writing is versatile and engaging. The squares can be used to record notes in categories, organize a report, sequence a narrative, or respond to literature. To create the squares, take a piece of paper, fold it in half, and then fold it in half again. Reopen it and draw lines on the fold lines to create four squares. Label each square with an element in the writing's organization. For example, the squares in Figure 8.5, a teaching chart from a unit on informational reports about animals, are labeled with categories of facts about rhinos: "live," "eat," "look like," and "do." The squares can be used for pictures and writing or just writing.

FIGURE 8.5 Teaching Chart for Four-Square Writing

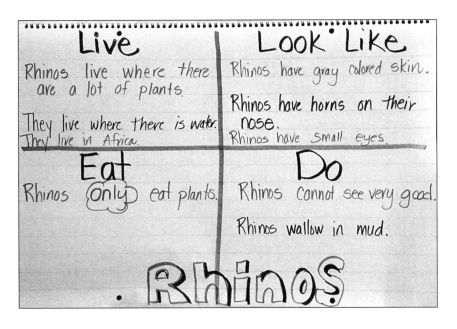

Appendix Listing

Minilesson Plan

Lesson Title _____ Objective _____

1. Connection	2. Direct Instruction
3. Engagement	
4. Closure	

List of 100 Most Frequently Used Words

the	or	will	number
of	one	up	no
and	had	other	way
a	by	about	would
to	word	out	people
in	but	many	my
is	not	then	than
you	what	them	first
that	all	these	water
it	were	so	been
he	we	some	call
was	when	her	who
for	your	would	am
on	can	make	its
are	said	like	now
as	there	him	gone
with	use	into	long
his	an	time	down
they	each	has	day
I	which	look	did
at	she	two	get
be	do	more	come
this	how	write	made
have	their	go	may
from	if	see	part

Adapted from Fry and Kress 2006.

© 2009 by Nancy Akhavan from *Teaching Writing in a Title I School, K–3*. Portsmouth, NH: Heinemann.

Appendix

Name _____

Date _____

My Writing

A–3

Name _____   Date _____

Title _____

_____

_____

_____

_____

_____

_____

_____

_____

_____

_____

_____

_____

_____

Name _____   Date _____

My Memory Moment

_____

_____

_____

_____

_____

_____

Name _____   Date _____

Editing

Editing Checklist

_____   I put capital letters at the beginning of sentences, the word "I", and the names of people.

_____   I put periods at the end of sentences.

_____   I can read my writing.

_____   My writing makes sense.

_____   If I drew a picture, the picture matches the words.

Name _____   Date _____

Planning

I visualized my memory moment. This is what happened:

FIRST

NEXT

THEN

LAST

Name _____   Date _____

Appendix

Page 2

Name _____   Date _____

Memory Moment

Think Small	Who	What/When/Where

_____

_____

_____

_____

_____

_____

_____

_____

_____

Name _____   Date _____

Add on-to Your Writing

To add on to your writing, first think about what you can add. Write those ideas down, and then revise your writing.

Beginning	I could add the following details: • detail • detail
Middle	I could add the following details: • detail • detail
End	I could add the following details: • detail • detail

Name _____   Date _____

♡ Favorite Part

Name _____   Date _____

_____

_____

_____

_____

_____

_____

_____

_____

_____

_____

Name _____   Date _____

Page 2

_____

_____

_____

_____

_____

_____

_____

_____

_____

use this additional page to add on to any writing paper

Copy and cut out this card and give it to students to remind them how to stretch words.

- - - - - - - - - - - - - - - - - - -

Bubblegum Stretch

We stretch words by saying them slowly and listening for the sounds we in hear in words. Then write down the sounds you hear.

Ready? Set? Stretch!

Say . . . the . . . word . . . slowly . . .
Listen . . . what do you hear?

- - - - - - - - - - - - - - - - - - -

Bubblegum Stretch

We stretch words by saying them slowly and listening for the sounds we in hear in words. Then write down the sounds you hear.

Ready? Set? Stretch!

Say . . . the . . . word . . . slowly . . .
Listen . . . what do you hear?

My Favorite Word Bank

Name _____

Write your favorite words in the boxes. Have a friend help you spell and check the word wall!

Name _____   Date _____

Use Pictures to Add Details

Draw pictures to tell your story in the box.

1. First,	2. Next,	3. Then,
4. After that,	5. Then,	6. Finally,

Name _____   Date _____

Nonfiction Notes

Today I read the book:

_____

I learned that

_____

_____

_____

_____

Picture

Name _____   Date _____

Nonfiction Notes

I read _____

by _____. From this book I learned

_____

_____

_____

_____

_____

_____

_____

Picture Word Card

Write the word in the box and then draw a picture to match the word.

Picture	Word

Picture	Word

Picture Word Bank

Name _____

Word	Picture
Word	Picture
Word	Picture
Word	Picture
Word	Picture

Name: _____

Type of Word _____

Examples:

Write the definition of the word type here:

_____

_____

_____

_____

_____

Word _____

Examples:

Write the definition of the word here:

_____
_____
_____
_____
_____

Words I Use

Name _____

My Spelling	Word Wall Spelling

Write your favorite words in the boxes. Have a friend help you spell and check by using the word wall!

Elkonian Box

A-24

Put the manipulative on the line, and when the child says the sound, have the child push the manipulative into the box.

© 2009 by Nancy Akhavan from *Teaching Writing in a Title I School, K–3*. Portsmouth, NH: Heinemann.

Appendix

References

Akhavan, Nancy. 2004. *How to Align Literacy Instruction, Assessment, and Standards and Achieve Results You Never Dreamed Possible.* Portsmouth, NH: Heinemann.

_____. 2007. *Accelerated Vocabulary Instruction.* New York: Scholastic.

_____. 2008. *The Title I Teacher's Guide to Teaching Reading, K–3.* Portsmouth, NH: Heinemann.

August, Diane, and Martha Vockley. 2002. *From Spanish to English: Reading and Writing for English Language Learners, Kindergarten Through Third Grade.* Pittsburgh: National Center on Education and the Economy.

Ball, Arnetha F. 2006. "Teaching Writing in Culturally Diverse Classrooms." In *Handbook of Writing Research*, ed. Charles A. MacArthur, Steve Graham, and Jill Fitzgerald, 293–310. New York: Guilford.

Barell, John. 2003. *Developing More Curious Minds.* Alexandria, VA: ASCD.

Bear, Donald R., Marcia Invernizzi, Shane Templeton, and Francine Johnston. 1996. *Words Their Way: Word Study for Phonics, Vocabulary, and Spelling.* Upper Saddle River, NJ: Prentice Hall.

Bender, Jenny Mechem. 2007. *The Resourceful Writing Teacher.* Portsmouth, NH: Heinemann.

Bereiter, Carol, and Marlene Scardamalia. 2006. "Education for the Knowledge Age: Design-Centered Models of Teaching and Instruction." In *Handbook of Educational Psychology*, 2d ed., ed. Patricia A. Alexander and Philip H. Winne, 695–714. Mahwah, NJ: Lawrence Erlbaum.

Berninger, Virginia W., and William D. Winn. 2006. "Implications of Advancements in Brain Research and Technology for Writing Development." In *Handbook of Writing Research*, ed. Charles A. MacArthur, Steve Graham, and Jill Fitzgerald 96–114. New York: Guilford.

Biemiller, Andrew. 1999. *Language and Reading Success.* Brookline, MA: Brookline Books.

Blankenstein, Alan. 2004. *Failure Is Not an Option.* Thousand Oaks, CA: Corwin.

Boscolo, Pietro, and Carmen Gelati. 2007. "Best Practices in Promoting Motivation for Writing." In *Best Practices in Writing Instruction*, ed. Steve Graham, Charles A. MacArthur, and Jill Fitzgerald 202—21. New York: Guilford.

Brewster, Cori, and Jennifer Fager. 2000. "Increasing Student Engagement and Motivation: From Time-on-Task to Homework." In *By Request* (October). Portland, OR: Northwest Regional Educational Laboratory.

Calkins, Lucy. 2003. *The Nuts and Bolts of Teaching Writing.* Portsmouth, NH: Heinemann.

Calkins, Lucy, and Stephanie Parsons. 2003. *Poetry: Powerful Thoughts in Tiny Packages*. Vol. 7, *Units of Study for Primary Writing*. Portsmouth, NH: Heinemann.

Cambourne, Brian. 2002. "Holistic, Integrated Approaches to Reading and Language Arts Instruction: The Constructivist Framework of an Instructional Theory." In *What Research Has to Say About Reading Instruction*, ed. Alan E. Farstrup and S. Jay Samuels, 25–47. Newark, DE: International Reading Association.

Chall, Jeanne S. 2000. *The Academic Achievement Challenge: What Really Works in the Classroom?* New York: Guilford.

Clay, Marie M. 2001. *Change Over Time in Children's Literacy Development*. Portsmouth, NH: Heinemann.

Csikszentmihalyi, M. 1990. *Flow: The Psychology of Optimal Experience*. New York: Harper and Row.

Cunningham, Patricia M., and James W. Cunningham. 2002. "What We Know About How to Teach Phonics." In *What Research Has to Say About Reading Instruction*, ed. Alan E. Farstrup and S. Jay Samuels, 87–109. Newark, DE: International Reading Association.

Donovan, Carol A., and Laura B. Smolkin. 2006. "Children's Understanding of Genre and Writing Development." In *Handbook of Writing Research*, ed. Charles A. MacArthur, Steve Graham, and Jill Fitzgerald, 131–43. New York: Guilford.

Dutro, Susana, and Carrol Moran. 2003. "Rethinking English Language Instruction: An Architectural Approach." In *English Learners: Reaching the Highest Level of English Literacy*, ed. Gilbert G. Garcia, 227–58. Newark, DE: International Reading Association.

Englert, Carol Sue, Troy V. Mariage, and Kailonnie Dunsmore. 2006. "Tenets of Sociocultural Theory in Writing Instruction Research." In *Handbook of Writing Research*, ed. Charles A. MacArthur, Steve Graham, and Jill Fitzgerald, 208–21. New York: Guilford.

Fisher, Douglas, and Nancy Frey. 2008. *Better Learning Through Structured Teaching: A Framework for the Gradual Release of Responsibility*. Alexandria, VA: ASCD.

Fletcher, Adam. 2008. "Students as Partners in Learning: Adam Fletcher Talks About Meaningful Student Involvement." *Northwest Education* 13 (3): 28–29.

Flores, Barbara, Patricia T. Cousin, and Esteban Diaz. 1991. "Critiquing and Transforming the Deficit Myths About Learning, Language, and Culture." *Language Arts* 68 (5): 369–79.

Fountas, Irene C., and Gay Su Pinnell. 1996. *Guided Reading: Good First Teaching for All Children*. Portsmouth, NH: Heinemann.

———. 2006. *Teaching for Comprehending and Fluency: Thinking, Talking, and Writing About Reading, K–8*. Portsmouth, NH: Heinemann.

Freeman, David, and Yvonne Freeman. 1998. *ESL/EFL Teaching: Principles for Success*. Portsmouth, NH: Heinemann.

Fry, Edward B., and Jacqueline E. Kress. 2006. *The Reading Teacher's Book of Lists*. 5th ed. San Francisco: Jossey-Bass.

Gibbons, Pauline. 2002. *Scaffolding Language, Scaffolding Learning: Teaching Second Language Learners in the Mainstream Classroom*. Portsmouth, NH: Heinemann.

Graham, Steve. 2006a. "Strategy Instruction and the Teaching of Writing." In *Handbook of Writing Research*, ed. Charles A. MacArthur, Steve Graham, and Jill Fitzgerald, 187–207. New York: Guilford.

———. 2006b. "Writing." In *Handbook of Educational Psychology*, 2d ed., ed. Patricia A. Alexander and Philip H. Winne, 457–78. Mahwah, NJ: Lawrence Erlbaum.

Graham, Steve, and Karen R. Harris. 2007. "Best Practices in Teaching Planning." In *Best Practices in Writing Instruction*, ed. Steve Graham, Charles A. MacArthur, and Jill Fitzgerald, 119–40. New York: Guilford.

Graham, Steve, Charles A. MacArthur, and Jill Fitzgerald. 2007. "Best Practices in Writing Instruction." In *Best Practices in Writing Instruction*, ed. Steve Graham, Charles A. MacArthur, and Jill Fitzgerald, 1–9. New York: Guilford.

Graves, Donald. 2003. *Writing: Teachers and Children at Work*. 20th anniv. ed. Portsmouth, NH: Heinemann.

Guthrie, John T., and Allan Wigfield. 2000. "Engagement and Motivation in Reading." In *Handbook of Reading Research*, vol. III, ed. Michael L. Kamil, Peter B. Mosenthal, P. David Pearson, and Rebecca Barr, 403–24. Mahwah, NJ: Lawrence Erlbaum.

Harris, Karen R., and Steve Graham. 1996. *Making the Writing Process Work: Strategies for Composition and Self-Regulation*. Brookline, MA: Brookline Books.

Haycock, Katy. 2001. "Closing the Achievement Gap." *Educational Leadership* 58 (6): 6–11.

Hidi, Suzanne, and Pietro Boscolo. 2006. "Motivation and Writing." In *Handbook of Writing Research*, ed. Charles A. MacArthur, Steve Graham, and Jill Fitzgerald, 144–57. New York: Guilford.

Hobbie, Holly. 2004. *Toot and Puddle: The New Friend*. New York: Little, Brown and Company.

Jensen, Eric. 2000. *Brain-Based Learning*. San Diego: Brain Store.

Krashen, Steven. 2003. *Explorations in Language Acquisition and Use*. Portsmouth, NH: Heinemann.

Maria, Katherine. 1998. "Developing Disadvantaged Children's Background Knowledge Interactively." In *Literacy Instruction for Culturally and Linguistically Diverse Students*, ed. Michael F. Opitz, 122–26. Newark, DE: International Reading Association.

Marzano, Robert J. 2004. "The Developing Vision of Vocabulary Instruction." In *Vocabulary Instruction: Research to Practice*, ed. James F. Baumann and Edward J. Kame'enui, 100–117. New York: Guilford.

McCutchen, Deborah. 2006. "Cognitive Factors in the Development of Children's Writing." In *Handbook of Writing Research,* ed. Charles A. MacArthur, Steve Graham, and Jill Fitzgerald, 115–30. New York: Guilford.

McKeough, Anne, Jaime Palmer, Marya Jarvey, and Stan Bird. 2007. "Best Narrative Writing Practices When Teaching from a Developmental Framework." In *Best Practices in Writing Instruction,* ed. Steve Graham, Charles A. MacArthur, and Jill Fitzgerald, 50–73. New York: Guilford.

Murray, Donald M. 2004. *A Writer Teaches Writing.* Rev. ed. Boston: Heinle and Heinle.

Nagy, William, E. 1988. *Teaching Vocabulary to Improve Reading Comprehension.* Newark, DE: International Reading Association.

National Writing Project and Carl Nagin. 2006. *Because Writing Matters: Improving Student Writing in Our Schools.* San Francisco: Jossey-Bass.

New Standards Primary Literacy Committee. 1999. *Reading and Writing Grade by Grade.* Pittsburgh: National Center on Education and the Economy.

New Standards Speaking and Listening Committee. 2001. *Speaking and Listening for Preschool Through Third Grade.* Pittsburgh: National Center on Education and the Economy.

Peregoy, Suzanne F., and Owen F. Boyle. 1999. "Multiple Embedded Scaffolds: Supporting English Learners' Social/Affective Linguistic and Academic Development in Kindergarten." *Kindergarten Education: Theory, Research, and Practice* 4 (1): 41–54.

Perry, Nancy E., Julianne C. Turner, and Debra K. Meyer. 2006. "Classrooms as Contexts for Motivating Learning." In *Handbook of Educational Psychology,* 2d ed., ed. Patricia A. Alexander and Philip H. Winne, 327–48. Mahwah, NJ: Lawrence Erlbaum.

Pressley, Michael, and Karen R. Harris. 2006. "Cognitive Strategies Instruction: From Basic Research to Classroom Instruction." In *Handbook of Educational Psychology,* 2d ed., ed. Patricia A. Alexander and Philip H. Winne, 265–86. Mahwah, NJ: Lawrence Erlbaum.

Pressley, Michael, Lindsey Mohan, Lauren Fingeret, Kelly Reffitt, and Lisa Raphael-Bogaert. 2007. "Writing Instruction in Engaging and Effective Elementary Settings." In *Best Practices in Writing Instruction,* ed. by Steve Graham, Charles A. MacArthur, and Jill Fitzgerald, 13–27. New York: Guilford.

Pritchard, Ruie J., and Ronald L. Honeycutt. 2006. "The Process Approach to Writing Instruction: Examining Its Effectiveness." In *Handbook of Writing Research,* ed. Charles A. MacArthur, Steve Graham, and Jill Fitzgerald, 275–92. New York: Guilford.

Rea, Denise M., and Sandra P. Mercuri. 2007. *Research-Based Strategies for English Language Learners: How to Reach Goals and Meet Standards, K–8.* Portsmouth, NH: Heinemann.

Rijlaarsdam, Gert, and Huub van den Bergh. 2006. "Writing Process Theory: A Functional Dynamic Approach." In *Handbook of Writing Research,* ed. Charles A. MacArthur, Steve Graham, and Jill Fitzgerald, 41–53. New York: Guilford.

Samway, Katharine Davies. 2006. *When English Language Learners Write: Connecting Research to Practice, K–8.* Portsmouth, NH: Heinemann.

Saphier, Jon, Mary Ann Haley-Speca, and Robert Gowen. 2008. *The Skillful Teacher: Building Your Teaching Strengths.* 6th ed. Acton, MA: Research for Better Teaching.

Schraw, Gregory. 2006. "Knowledge Structures and Processes." In *Handbook of Educational Psychology,* ed. Patricia A. Alexander and Philip H. Winne, 245–64. Mahwah, NJ: Lawrence Erlbaum.

Schunk, Dale H., and Barry J. Zimmerman. 2006. "Competence and Control Beliefs: Distinguishing the Means and Ends." In *Handbook of Educational Psychology,* 2d. ed., ed. Patricia A. Alexander and Philip H. Winne, 349–68. Mahwah, NJ: Lawrence Erlbaum.

Sinatra, Richard, Jeffrey S. Beaudry, Josephine Stahl-Gemake, and E. Francine Guastello. 1998. "Combining Visual Literacy, Text Understanding, and Writing for Culturally Diverse Students." In *Literacy Instruction for Culturally and Linguistically Diverse Students,* ed. Michael F. Opitz, 173–79. Newark, DE: International Reading Association.

Skinner, E., and M. Belmont. 1991. A Longitudinal Study of Motivation in School: Reciprocal Effects of Teacher Behavior and Student Engagement. Unpub. ms. Rochester, NY: University of Rochester.

Spandel, Vicki. 2005. *The Nine Rights of Every Writer: A Guide for Teachers.* Portsmouth, NH: Heinemann.

———. 2008. *Creating Young Writers: Using the Six Traits to Enrich Writing Process in Primary Classrooms.* Boston: Pearson Education.

Stahl, Steven. 1999. *Vocabulary Development.* Brookline, MA: Brookline Books.

Stahl, Steven, and William E. Nagy. 2006. *Teaching Word Meanings.* Mahwah, NJ: Lawrence Erlbaum.

Stiggins, Richard J., Judith A. Arter, Jan Chappuis, and Stephen Chappuis. 2004. *Classroom Assessment for Student Learning: Doing It Right—Using It Well.* Portland, OR: Assessment Training Institute.

Strickland, Dorothy S. 1998. "Educating African American Learners at Risk: Finding a Better Way." In *Literacy Instruction for Culturally and Linguistically Diverse Students,* ed. Michael F. Opitz, 71–80. Newark, DE: International Reading Association.

Tompkins, Gail E. 1997. *Literacy for the 21st Century: A Balanced Approach.* Upper Saddle River, NJ: Prentice Hall.

Vygotsky, Lev. 1978. *Mind in Society: The Development of Higher Psychological Processes.* Cambridge, MA: Harvard University Press.

Wiggins, Grant, and Jay McTighe. 1998. *Understanding by Design.* Alexandria, VA: Association for Supervision and Curriculum Development.

Index

Teaching *Reading* in a **TITLE I** School, K–3

In *Teaching Reading in a Title I School*, **Nancy Akhavan**, a Title I principal, takes a pragmatic approach to meeting reading benchmarks. She provides encouraging, practical advice and classroom-tested solutions with a focus on what's really important in helping struggling students. You'll find doable solutions to instructional problems, and you'll connect your professional learning to your students' learning.

You understand the obstacles. Now learn how to overcome them. Read *Teaching Reading in a Title I School* and take the advice of a Title I veteran. You'll find proven ways to help your students grow into lifelong readers and to help your school exceed expectations.

978-0-325-01083-0 / 2008 / 224 pp/ $25.00

Sample Chapters
available online
www.heinemann.com

PD Heinemann Professional Development

Through Heinemann Professional Development you can experience **Nancy Akhavan**'s powerful ideas in person. Book Nancy Akhavan as a speaker for your upcoming event.

For information on the full range of professional development options, including:

- Speaking engagements
- On-site seminars
- Off-site workshops
- Multiday institutes

Visit pd.heinemann.com

TO ORDER CALL **800.225.5800** OR VISIT **www.heinemann.com**

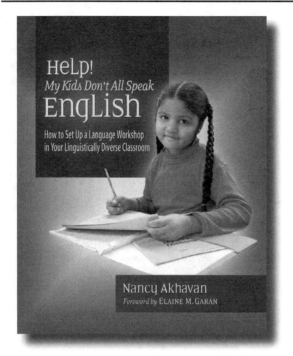